The Maker's Mark

The Maker's Mark

THE COWBOY'S DEVOTIONAL

Beau Hague

Copyright © 2019 by Beau Hague

All rights reserved. No part of this publication may be reproduced, distributed, or transmitted in any form or by any means, including photocopying, recording, or other electronic or mechanical methods, without the prior written permission of the publisher, except in the case of brief quotations embodied in critical reviews and certain other noncommercial uses permitted by copyright law. For permission requests, write to the publisher at the address below.

Fedd Books
P.O. Box 341973
Austin, TX 78734
www.thefeddagency.com

Published in association with The Fedd Agency, Inc., a literary agency.

Unless otherwise noted, all scripture quotations are taken from the Holy Bible, New International Version®, NIV®. Copyright © 1973, 1978, 1984, 2011 by Biblica, Inc.™ Used by permission of Zondervan. All rights reserved worldwide. www.zondervan.com The "NIV" and "New International Version" are trademarks registered in the United States Patent and Trademark Office by Biblica, Inc.™

Scripture quotations marked (NLT) are taken from the Holy Bible, New Living Translation, copyright ©1996, 2004, 2015 by Tyndale House Foundation. Used by permission of Tyndale House Publishers, Inc., Carol Stream, Illinois 60188. All rights reserved.

Scripture quotations marked (ESV) are taken from the ESV® Bible (The Holy Bible, English Standard Version®), copyright © 2001 by Crossway, a publishing ministry of Good News Publishers. Used by permission. All rights reserved.

Scripture quotations marked (NASB) are taken from the New American Standard Bible® (NASB), Copyright © 1960, 1962, 1963, 1968, 1971, 1972, 1973, 1975, 1977, 1995 by The Lockman Foundation. Used by permission. www.Lockman.org

Scripture quotations marked KJV are taken from the King James Version of the Bible.

Day 4: *This Old Horse.* "Doc Bar." Episode 5. Directed by Nathan Fletcher. Ride TV, January 14, 2015.
Day 6: *Rio Bravo* directed by Howard Hanks (Warner Bros. 1959.), Film.
Day 10: *8 Seconds* directed by John G. Avildsen (New Line Cinema. 1994.), Film.
Day 16: Evans, Jimmy. *The Right One.* HarperCollins, 2015.
Day 36: Franklin, Jentezen. *Love Like You've Never Been Hurt.* Chosen, 2018.
Day 38: American Cowboy. "Texas Titans." American Cowboy | Western Lifestyle - Travel - People, 1 Nov. 2017, www.americancowboy.com/people/texas-frontier-titans-lone-star-state-history.
Day 38: *Lonesome Dove* directed by Wincer Simon (CBS. 1989.), Television.
Day 39: "The Cowboys" directed by Mark Rydell (Warner Bros,1972.), Film.
Day 40: *Pure Country* directed by Christopher Cain (Warner Bros. 1992.), Film.

Cover Photo by Beau Hague/H Brand Photography

ISBN: 978-1-949784-14-5
eISBN: 978-1-949784-15-2

Printed in the United States of America
First Edition 15 14 13 12 11 / 10 9 8 7 6 5 4 3 2

This book is dedicated to all the mentors in my life. Each of your investments in my life as a follower of Christ and/or cowboy has made me the man that I am today.

Kent and Crickette Hague
Larry Bolton
Andy Bolton
Billy and Vici-Beth Morgan
Rick and Cathy Whitaker
Kreg and Donna Murphree
Ron and Norma Cline
Doug and Lana Melton
Odus and Paula-K Compton
Mickey and Elva Bentley
David and Karen Gray
Marshall Long

Contents

Introduction xiii

THE MAKER'S MARK 17
Day 1 *(Genesis 1:27)*

BUD BOX 22
Day 2 *(John 1:14)*

THE SWEAT RING 25
Day 3 *(Colossians 3:23)*

THE DOC BAR LEGACY 29
Day 4 *(Psalm 78:4)*

HANK'S FIRST SHOT 33
Day 5 *(James 4:8)*

RIO BRAVO 36
Day 6 *(John 12:43)*

HELL KNOW 40
Day 7 *(Romans 8:1)*

THE MENTAL GAME 43
Day 8 *(Proverbs 23:7)*

FIGHT WITH A TEXAS RANGER *47*
Day 9 *(Ephesians 5:16)*

TRAVELIN' PARTNERS *51*
Day 10 *(Proverbs 13:20)*

MADELINE'S FIRST DRIVE *55*
Day 11 *(Romans 12:11)*

GET OFF ON THE PAIN *59*
Day 12 *(1 Timothy 6:17)*

WASTED *63*
Day 13 *(Ephesians 5:11)*

OPEN ANOTHER GATE *67*
Day 14 *(1 Corinthians 9:22)*

CAN YOU STILL ROPE? *71*
Day 15 *(2 Corinthians 4:17)*

THE BIRDS AND THE BULLS *76*
Day 16 *(Genesis 2:25)*

THE BIRDS AND THE BULLS: PART 2 .... *81*
Day 17 *(1 Thessalonians 4:3-5)*

TIED ON GREEN *86*
Day 18 *(Romans 12:3)*

USING GEAR *90*
Day 19 *(Ephesians 2:10)*

DEAD OR ALIVE *94*
Day 20 *(2 Corinthians 10:4)*

DOUBLE-WIDE BLESSING *98*
Day 21 *(Joshua 1:8)*

SHRINK *103*
Day 22 *(Hebrews 10:39)*

LOSING MY RELIGION *108*
Day 23 *(Galatians 6:7)*

ARE YOU OPEN? *111*
Day 24 *(1 John 1:9 and Matthew 7:16)*

BUCKED OFF BARON *115*
Day 25 *(Luke 15:20)*

FARM WELD *120*
Day 26 *(Colossians 1:17)*

RELENTLESS *124*
Day 27 *(Matthew 5:6 and Luke 16:10)*

WE CALL HIM FINGERS *128*
Day 28 *(Luke 18:14)*

THE UNDERDOG *132*
Day 29 *(Luke 18:27 and Ephesians 3:20)*

WALKING ON A LOOSE REIN *136*
Day 30 *(Mark 5:27, 29)*

LISTEN TO YOUR ASS *141*
Day 31 *(Numbers 22:28)*

GRIT DON'T QUIT *145*
Day 32 *(2 Chronicles 15:7)*

THE GOOD OLD DAYS *150*
Day 33 *(Ecclesiastes 7:10)*

SHIFT HAPPENS *154*
Day 34 *(Philippians 1:12)*

STRIPPING PERFECTION *157*
Day 35 *(Philippians 3:12)*

FORGIVING MY COWGIRL *163*
Day 36 *(1 Corinthians 13:7)*

PURPLE SOCK *168*
Day 37 *(Acts 20:35)*

THE SCOUT *171*
Day 38 *(Deuteronomy 31:8)*

HERD ANIMALS 175
Day 39 *(Romans 12:15-16)*

KING GEORGE'S ENCORE 179
Day 40 *(1 Corinthians 2:9)*

Notes...183

Introduction

Thank you so much for picking up this book. I've had the pleasure of working on some of the best ranches in Northwest Oklahoma and West Texas with some of the best cowboys in the country. It's out of these experiences day-working and pastoring for over two decades that I've written this devotional.

In Volume 2 of the *The Cowboy's Devotional* series, *The Maker's Mark: The Cowboy's Devotional,* we'll dig deeper into understanding God's will for your life. By extending the readings a bit and being a little more vulnerable, I pray that you will find even more meaning and strength from this book than you did in the first one. My prayer is that the Lord would use each story and His word to grow you into the person that He wants you to be. I pray that you know that our Maker, the God of the Universe,

The Maker's Mark

through His Son Jesus, has left an eternal mark on you. A mark of salvation and eternal life. A mark through which you can find strength and power through the work of the Holy Spirit. I pray that you would feel the Spirit of God moving not only in you but also through you, helping you make an eternal impact in the world around you. It's my prayer that every person that reads these pages would know that knowledge is not the goal... application is. We should desire to apply what we learn so that we can leave a mark on this world that will last for eternity.

As you begin this ride, I encourage you to pray before you read each day's reading. Ask God to reveal Himself through what you're about to read. Ask for something new, something fresh and powerful. Ask Him to strengthen you to actually do what He reveals to you each day. Then read that day's reading, honestly answering the "Chew on This" questions, and making a prayerful commitment to live out what God reveals to you that day. I'm believing that you will be inspired by what the Lord can do when you consistently spend time praying and reading His Word.

CHEW ON THIS

One of my favorite verses in the Bible is Joshua 1:8, "Do not let this book of the law depart from your mouth;

Introduction

meditate on it day and night, that you may be careful to do everything written in it—then you will be prosperous and successful." My dad calls it the "key to success," because if we choose to meditate on the Word of God, God promises we will succeed.

What does it mean to meditate on God's Word? I'll illustrate it by using the example of a cow chewing its cud. A cow has four stomachs, and she will graze out in the pasture eating grass or hay. Once she does that, a cow will usually lay down and chew her cud. This process includes chewing the grass up, swallowing it, getting some nutrients from the forage, and then regurgitating it up and chewing it again. Cows will do this many times and each time they chew, swallow, and regurgitate their food, they are gaining the nutrients from the food and growing.

Meditating on the Word of God is just like chewing cud. We take in God's Word into our heart, mind, and soul by reading it. Once we've taken it in, we are told to meditate or chew on its truth and allow it to fill our heart. If we chew on God's Word through the process of reading it, thinking on it, and applying its powerful truths, it will help us grow in our spiritual lives each day! Psalm 1:1-2 says, "Blessed is the one who does not walk in step with the wicked or stand in the way that sinners take or sit in the company of mockers, but whose delight is in the law of the Lord, and who meditates on his law day and night."

The Maker's Mark

My prayer is that you would be blessed and grow in your life with your Maker as you chew on His Word daily.

PRAYER

Prayer is the privilege of every follower of Christ to talk personally with God. At the end of each devotion, you will be given a suggested prayer. I hope that you will tap into the power of God by praying these prayers of commitment. Remember, if we want to experience what only God can do, then we have to ask. Psalm 116:1-2 says, "I love the Lord because he hears my voice and my prayer for mercy. Because he bends down to listen, I will pray as long as I have breath!" (NLT).

DAY 1

The Maker's Mark

GENESIS 1:27

So God created human beings in his own image. In the image of God he created them; male and female he created them. (NLT)

When it comes to quality gear like saddles, spurs, buckles, and bits, all of these have one thing in common: they all have a *maker's mark*. What is a maker's mark? It's most commonly the maker's name, brand, or logo that is stamped somewhere on their gear. This is done to show that they are the ones who made the gear and that they are proud of what they've made.

This maker's mark is especially important to cowboys, because in a lot of cases who made the gear is what

The Maker's Mark

gives it its value. For example, if you have a bit or pair of spurs with the name Klapper stamped on them, you have something that is fairly valuable. Why? Because the man who made them is none other than the world-renowned bit and spur maker Billy Klapper. Another example would be if you have anything made of rawhide by Luis Ortega, you have something made by a master. Luis's mark is the style in which he braids. It's often referred to as California tradition, and if you know what you're looking for, you can spot his mark from a mile away. The other interesting thing about having gear made by a master is that, in many cases, it doesn't matter what condition the gear is in, it still holds its value when it's made by a master maker. In other words, heavily used gear can still be priceless if it has a maker's mark from a master in the craft.

If we were being honest, I think we'd all have to admit that we often try to find our value in the things of this world. Things like how well we do our job; how broke our horse is; if we're married, single, or dating. Or maybe we try and find our value in how well our kids perform in sports, how much money we have, or even how many likes we got on our last social media post. I know for me, I can often search for my value in how many people listen to my talks online, how cool people think my photos are, or how many books I've sold. Well, if you haven't figured it out yet, this is a miserable way to live. Why? Because

The Maker's Mark

the world we live in is so fickle, finding our value in what we have, what we've accomplished, or what people think about us is so unstable. This is why it's important to find our value in the one who made us. Who am I speaking of? I'm talking about the Divine Maker, the Master Craftsman of Mankind, the World-Renowned Creator of all things, —GOD ALMIGHTY.

You may be thinking, "Where's my Maker's mark? Is it that birthmark on my butt?" No, it's not. And please don't ever mention that birthmark on your butt again. The answer is . . . YOU. You are the Maker's mark. Don't miss this! Because we were created in the image of God, because we have a soul—because He's made every one of us unique and one of a kind—we are our Maker's mark! Every human to walk the face of this earth is given the mark of our Maker at conception, and, because of this, we are our Maker's most valuable creation.

How do I know? Because God showed us that we are worth more than life itself. John 3:16 says, "For God so loved the world that he gave his one and only son, that whosoever believes in him, shall not perish but have eternal life." Did you hear how much He loves you and me? God loved us so much that He allowed His one and only Son, Jesus, to be crucified for our sin. That's how much God values us. And guess what? He didn't do that for anything else He created, just for us!

The Maker's Mark

You may be reading this and thinking, "Surely God loves those church-going, good people who don't cuss or chew, or date girls who do, more than He loves me. And surely I have to do something to deserve His mark." Well, if you're thinking this, you're thinking is wrong. God placed His worth on us before we ever deserved it. Romans 5:8 says, "But God showed his great love for us by sending Christ to die for us **while we were still sinners**" (NLT). This verse tells us that even though we were scarred with sin, used and abused, God saw worth in what He made and proved it by paying the ultimate price—the death of His Son. And unlike the things of this world, when it comes to our value in God's eyes, *our value never changes*. Despite what we've done or not done, despite how well we've performed or not performed, God's love for you has never changed and never will.

But there's a catch. I know, I know, you're thinking, "Crap . . . I knew there had to be a catch!" Well, it's not what you're thinking. The catch is that to really understand our worth, we must place our trust in our Maker's Son (i.e. Jesus). John 1:12 says, "But to all who believed him and accepted him, he gave the right to become children of God" (NLT).

See, although our worth was settled on the cross, God gives us a *choice* to believe in Him and accept His gift of eternal life. How do we accept this gift? We give our lives

The Maker's Mark

to Jesus. It's only in doing this that we will ever truly find our true worth and personally know our Maker.

CHEW ON THIS
What do you find yourself trying to find your worth in? How have you let people or things determine your value? Do you feel worthless and beat up today? Why or why not? Have you given your life to Jesus?

PRAYER
Dear Jesus, I'm tired of trying to find my worth in this world. Forgive me for looking anywhere else but you to find my value. I'm accepting your gift of salvation and giving you ownership of my life. Thank you for making me and paying the ultimate price so that I could be saved.

DAY 2

Bud Box

JOHN 1:14
The Word became flesh and made his dwelling among us. We have seen his glory, the glory of the one and only Son, who came from the Father, full of grace and truth.

If you've ever worked cattle in a set of pens that weren't set up right, you know how it can make for a long, frustrating day. What do I mean by pens that aren't set up right? Well, good pens are built in a way that cattle want to naturally move in the direction you're trying to take them. For example, if the holding pen isn't set up for getting cattle sorted and into the lane, it's no good. If the lane is too wide and cattle can get by you fairly easily, this is also no bueno. If the crowding pen/tub isn't built right, cattle can push the tub gate back on you or just circle in a cloud of dust, leading to a log jam of hot cattle and hot

Bud Box

cowboys.

Because I've experienced these issues more than once while working on other ranches, when it came to building my own set of pens, I decided to build a *bud box*. What is a bud box? Well it's a box/tub that was designed by a guy named Bud. In our setup, it's a 14' x 20' rectangular shaped pen at the end of a long lane. What makes it special is that the gate you close behind you once you and the cattle are in the box is a solid gate set at an angle leading directly into the working chute. So, when the cattle enter the box, they hit the far end and instinctively want to turn around and go back the way they came. Knowing this, all I have to do is walk to one side of the box and let them roll back naturally in the direction they came from. When they do this, they hit the solid gate that is set on the angle, leading them through the opening and into the working chute. The bud box uses a cow's natural instinct to get them to go where you want them to go, and, from my experience, it works.

Similarly, when it comes to being the church, I believe that for us to continue to reach those far from God with the Good News of Jesus, we must live our lives in a way that naturally draws people to Christ. An example of this would be love. Love naturally softens people's hearts to hear the gospel. Another example would be showing the world what we stand for, not just what we stand against.

The Maker's Mark

Or offering grace instead of guilt. Giving to others instead of expecting them to give to us. All these things naturally open doors (or gates) for the gospel to be shared. All throughout scripture, we see that Jesus constantly changed His method to reach the lost while never compromising the truth. And guess what? It worked!

CHEW ON THIS
Are you living in a way that naturally draws people to Christ? Or does the way you live make it hard for them to know Him? How can you rebuild your approach or setup to reach more people for Christ? What ministry can you start or team can you join that will reach those far from God?

PRAYER
God, give me the wisdom to know how to draw people to you. May you use me to tear down any obstacles that keep others from your love.

DAY 3

The Sweat Ring

COLOSSIANS 3:23
Whatever you do, work at it with all your heart, as working for the Lord, not for human masters.

I love wearing a cowboy hat. My choice, whether it's straw or felt, is a Texas puncher crease with a 5" brim. I tell people that I wear the 5" brim because it makes me look skinnier. It's true . . . you don't have to lose weight to look skinnier, just buy a bigger brimmed hat (that's some free advice from your personal fashion expert . . . me). Whether it's the Cattleman's crease, Puncher, Gus, Cutter, or even the Dale Yeah, the different styles and shapes of cowboy hats are endless. Anyone wearing one can show his or her authentic style in the hat they wear.

The Maker's Mark

I've had many cowboy hats over the years because, unfortunately, I've had to retire a few. I say "had to" because, well, my wife told me I had to, and, secondly, they got to where even I couldn't stand to wear them. Why? Because they stunk! I didn't notice it at first, but I remember the first time I really smelled it. I'd taken a shower and gotten dressed, and, as I brought my hat toward my head to put it on, the smell about made me barf. The smell came from the sweat ring that had formed around the hatband, and, though I can't prove this, I think it was alive. What caused the smell, you might ask? It was from the dirt, cow snot, smoke, dust, rain, and sweat that came from working in the Oklahoma heat.

I know this may sound weird, but since I was a kid I've received so much pleasure from hard work. Sure, I've had days where I just wanted to chill and do nothing, but most days I enjoyed hard work, whether it was mowing the yard or bucking hay. Even now when people ask me what I do for fun, I've been known to reply, "manual labor." See, my father and mother intentionally and inherently passed on their work ethic to their boys, and for that I'm eternally grateful. I now have made it one of my goals to teach my kids the blessing of hard work. Why is this so important to me? It's because I believe that it not only assures that they will have food to eat, but it also brings God pleasure. I honestly believe that God

The Sweat Ring

gets excited when He sees us not only pray for His provision and blessing but when we also do our part to make it happen. The advice that I give my kids and that I would give anyone is: *Don't pray for things you're not willing to work for.* For example, you might be praying to one day be married. Don't pray for a spouse unless you're willing to work at making your marriage great. Trust me, it's awesome, but it takes work. Maybe you desire to grow your cattle operation, start a new business, or win the big game. Understand that it takes both praying as though everything depends on God, and working as though everything depends on you.

Unfortunately, so many people want the success without the sweat ring. They want to experience "overnight success." I would argue that most truly successful people became successful because they chose to get down on their knees daily, asking God to be the center of every area of their lives, and then they got off their knees and went to work for it. From my experience, one without the other usually leads to disappointment. I've known people that pray a lot but don't do the work, then they end up disappointed because nothing happens. I've also known people who are workaholics, but they don't center their lives on Jesus and when they reach the top, they find themselves empty and alone.

The truth is, without God at the center of it, work is

just that: work. But when we live by the words in our key verse and do our work as working for the Lord, this gives our efforts a whole new meaning. Instead of focusing on making money and spending it, we tend to focus on how we can invest our money in causes that matter. We work harder and find more fulfillment, because what we are doing is changing lives. So, what are you working for? Is it just to make money and die? Or is it to bring God glory through the time and sweat you put in? John 6:27 says it well, "Do not work for food that spoils, but for food that endures to eternal life, which the Son of Man will give you . . ."

CHEW ON THIS
When was the last time you sweat for the Lord? What's something you're doing right now that is making a difference in eternity? What can you change to make your work more eternally focused? How are you training your kids to find pleasure in hard work?

PRAYER
Lord Jesus, help me to not waste my time working for things that don't last. I want to bring you glory through my work, so show me how I can work in a way that changes eternity. I give you everything.

DAY 4

The Doc Bar Legacy

PSALM 78:4
We will not hide these truths from our children; we will tell the next generation about the glorious deeds of the LORD, about his power and his mighty wonders. (NLT)

I recently watched a documentary on the famous cutting horse Sire Doc Bar. Foaled in 1956, Doc Bar gave hopes to the Finley Ranch in Arizona of another racing champion. He had the look of a winner and he came from great racing bloodlines. But his racing career proved to be an epic failure after four races with winnings of only ninety-five dollars. Having great conformation and good looks, the owners chose to try him in the halter class. Doc Bar's conformation and style soon changed what judges

The Maker's Mark

looked for in a great halter horse. Out of the fifteen halter horse events that Doc Bar was shown in, he won nine grand championships and one reserve championship. It was at the height of his success in the halter horse industry that his owners decided to retire him and concentrate on Doc Bar's future as a stud. This began his real legacy as a performance horse sire.

Believing that Doc Bar possessed the traits that could change yet another part of the horse industry, his owners began training Doc Bar's foals and showing them in the cutting horse events. Doc Bar went on to sire famous offspring such as Doc O'Lena and grand-get Smart Little Lena, among many other great horses. His offspring have become National Cutting Horse Futurity champions, and many have become world champions. His ability to pass on his amazing talent was shown in 1983, when twenty-one out of the twenty-three finalists at the NCHA Futurity carried Doc Bar's blood. His offspring have gone on to receive tens of millions of dollars in earnings. As I watched this documentary about this amazing horse, what stood out to me most was not all the things that he accomplished himself in the show ring, but how much success the horses that he sired had following him. The fact is, Doc Bar changed the cutting horse industry like no other horse has, and he never once showed in a cutting horse event. That astounds me.

The Doc Bar Legacy

I heard a pastor say one time, "Our greatest legacy is not what we do, but who we raise." I know for myself, there have been times in my life where I've focused much of my time and energy on what I could accomplish as a leader in the church. I've given the church my best and have, in many ways, fallen short as a husband and father. At times, I've neglected teaching and leading my own children to live for Christ. And to be honest, I still struggle with putting ministry and others ahead of my family.

The truth is, I've been given the honor of raising three wonderful kids, and God has revealed to me that they are my greatest legacy. Sure, I'm called to make a difference at my job and lead people to a relationship with Jesus, but my first calling is to pass on to my daughter and sons a spiritual legacy that will outlast us all. I'm called to raise them to love Jesus with all their hearts, to teach them to love and live by His Word, to show them what it looks like to love your spouse and raise a godly family. Doc Bar's lasting legacy isn't based on what he did but who he raised. We should want the same to be said of us.

CHEW ON THIS

Are you more focused on *what* you *do,* than *who* God has entrusted you to raise? Are you chasing a title or a dream that won't last? It's time to ask God to turn your focus to what really matters in life, to help you lead your family well and leave a legacy that will last for eternity.

PRAYER

Lord, show me where my true focus is. I don't want to leave an earthly legacy that won't last. I want to leave an eternal legacy and I want it to start with my own children. Give me the strength, energy, and commitment I need to raise kids that love and serve you.

DAY 5

Hank's First Shot

JAMES 4:8
Come close to God, and God will come close to you . . . (NLT)

One of the highlights of living on a ranch or knowing someone who owns land is that you get to go hunting. Whether it's hunting duck, deer, quail, turkey, or even sandhill crane (ribeye of the sky), it's all a blast. So, when my son Hank said he wanted to go deer hunting, I got very excited. He was about eight years old at the time and had never been hunting before. So, because he needed a gun his size, we went gun shopping and bought him a Savage 223 youth model. It was just the right size and caliber for Hank to learn on. Soon after we bought it, we went out to sight it in and let Hank get used to shooting it. When it came time to shoot it for the first time, just like most young kids that have never shot a rifle before, Hank got a little scared. So, to show him that it wasn't

The Maker's Mark

going to hurt him, I loaded it and shot it first. Seeing that it really didn't kick and that it wasn't that loud, he felt more comfortable, so I loaded the gun again and handed it to him. After a minute or two of trying to find the target in the scope, he finally said he could see the target. I then coached him on how the bullseye on the target needs to be right in the center of the crosshairs. "I've got it on the bullseye," he said, so I told him to take the safety off and slowly pull the trigger. He began to tear up, and he softly whispered, "I'm scared."

I love my son, and he knows that I wouldn't intentionally hurt him, but he was still scared to shoot it because he thought it might hurt when it kicked. Being the dad that wants to raise tough sons, I tried to convince him that it wasn't going to hurt—he just needed to pull the trigger. Well, no matter what I told him, he didn't want to do it. Finally, he looked at me with tears in his eyes and said, "I'll shoot it if you'll just get close to me." So, I knelt down next to him, put my arm on his arm, and held him close. He pulled the trigger instantly. The tears stopped, and a smile of joy filled his face.

Much like my son, I think if we were to get really honest, we would all have to admit that we get scared sometimes. It could be because we have a big test and we need to make a good grade. Or fear sets in when we get laid off at our job and we don't know how we're going to pay the

Hank's First Shot

bills. Maybe we're sick and don't know what the future is going to be like. Well, just like my son asked me to get close because he was scared, I believe that, in our time of fear, God wants us to turn to Him and ask Him to come close to us. Remember, God is just a prayer away.

CHEW ON THIS

What are you fearful of right now? What is causing you to worry? Have you asked God for help? Have you asked Him to come close to you? Don't wait another second. Ask for Him to come near to you and make His presence known, so that you can face your fears with His strength.

PRAYER

Lord, I'm scared. I don't know what to do, so I'm turning to you right now and asking you to come close to me and take away my fear. I want my decisions to be based on faith, not fear. Thank you for always being with me no matter what I face in this life.

DAY 6

Rio Bravo

JOHN 12:43
For they loved human praise more than praise from God.

In the movie *Rio Bravo,* John Wayne plays sheriff John T. Chance, and Dean Martin plays Chance's friend Dude. Dude is the town drunk turned sheriff's deputy. During an altercation between a drunk Dude and the movie's bad guy, Joe Burdette, Burdette shoots an innocent man, landing him in jail. For the rest of the movie, Chance, Dude, and Stumpy—the jail keeper played by the great Walter Brennan—do what they can to keep Burdette jailed while fighting off Burdette's brother and his men.

While Chance and Dude are the main characters of this great western, I'd say there's another character that, in my opinion, steals the show. His name is Colorado Ryan. Played by real-life Rock and Roll Hall of Famer

Rio Bravo

Ricky Nelson, Colorado is a young gunslinger hired by Chance's friend Pat Wheeler to protect his wagons and cargo. Knowing that Sheriff Chance needs some help fighting off Burdette's men, Wheeler suggests Chance hire Colorado. Wheeler tells Chance, "he's good . . . real good." Trusting his friend's advice and knowing Colorado's reputation as a fast-draw, Chance asks Colorado to be his deputy. Colorado kindly turns him down, claiming what he's better at is, "minding my own business." But after Wheeler is shot and killed by Burdette's men, Colorado decides to give in to Chance's request and become a deputy. In one scene of the movie, Chance, Dude, and Stumpy are having a conversation about Colorado, when Dude asks Chance, "I wonder if he's as good as Wheeler said?" To which Chance replies, "I'd say he is. I'd say he's so good that he doesn't feel he has to prove it."

I think all of us who deal with pride find ourselves constantly being tempted to prove ourselves to others. We do things like post our latest purchase, our latest accomplishment, or latest win while secretly hoping people will notice. We think that if we can get enough hits on our website, subscribers on our YouTube channel, or hearts on our Instagram post, it will prove to the world that we matter. We mistakenly believe that, through a like, a heart, or a comment, we will somehow prove that we are valuable.

The Maker's Mark

If you're like me, and you've found yourself caught in this act, you know how empty you feel when you don't get the response you were hoping for. While sharing how God's blessed us or used us isn't always a sin, I would argue that feeling like we have to do certain things or act a certain way to prove our worth to others is a sick cycle that most often leads to disappointment. See, Colorado didn't have to draw his gun to prove he was a good shot. He just did his job, served others, and let everyone think what they wanted.

God has given us all gifts and talents to use for His glory, and we should never apologize for how He uses us to make a difference in this world. But what we must do is examine our hearts and motives to make sure that what we are doing is done out of our love for God and others. When our motive is right and our desire is to bring God glory, we will find lasting fulfillment while doing the things that we are good at.

CHEW ON THIS

What is one thing you've done or are doing to try to impress others? Ask God to expose your motives and purify your intentions so that He can receive the praise and honor that He deserves. Then get out there and enjoy using the gifts God has given you to serve others and make an eternal difference.

PRAYER

God, please purify my motives. Help me not to live to please others or feel that I have to prove myself to anyone. Forgive me for where I've promoted myself over you, and use the things that I'm good at to bring you glory and help change the world.

DAY 7

Hell Know

ROMANS 8:1

Therefore, there is now no condemnation for those who are in Christ Jesus.

I know that I'm not the only one who has bad days, but sometimes I have days where it seems like anything that could go wrong, does. Days that if they were a fish, I'd definitely throw them back. Days when your cows get out on the coldest day of winter. Or a rainstorm washes your water gap out again. Or that weld you put on that gate breaks loose when you're right in the middle of working cattle. If you're a parent, you may have days when your kids seem like they're possessed by the demon of whining. Or maybe your "so-called" friends at school decide that you're no longer cool enough to sit at their table for lunch.

Trying situations seem to happen more often than not,

Hell Know

and it sometimes feels like they're happening all at once. So, the question is: how do we get through these painful trials here on earth? Well, one of the things I've learned is that most of life isn't about what happens to us, but how we think about what happens to us. If I let it, life can really discourage me. If I focus on my failures and losses, I can really get to thinking about how bad things are. But if I re-frame my circumstances with the frame of hope, gratefulness, and joy, then I can see my circumstances in a totally different light. Instead of hating that the cows got out again, I can turn that thought on its ear and think, "God, thank you for giving me these cows to help provide for my family." Instead of cursing the rain that washed out the water gap, I can think thoughts like, "Praise God we got rain because without it, the grass would not grow, and I wouldn't be able to make a living." Instead of griping about how that weld didn't hold, I can praise God for the physical ability to open a gate with my own two hands. And when the kids are having a whine fest, I can be grateful that I have healthy kids that are alive and well.

The truth is, life is hell sometimes, but if we've placed our trust and hope in Jesus, then this earth is the only hell we'll ever know—praise God.

CHEW ON THIS
What are you cussing right now that you need to re-frame

how you think about it? What event or circumstance are you facing right now that is stealing your faith in God? Ask God to change the way you think and give you a new way of seeing the trials you face. Remember, much of life isn't about what happens to us, but how we think about what happens to us.

PRAYER
God, change the way I think about life. Give me hope even when all hell is breaking loose around me. I thank you that, because of your sacrifice on the cross, this earth is the only hell that I will ever know.

DAY 8

The Mental Game

PROVERBS 23:7
For as he thinks within himself, so he is . . . (NASB)

Brent Lewis is a rodeo legend. He's been an NFR qualifier in the tie down roping eleven times, with earnings of over $1.5 million and counting. Not only is he a great roper, he's a great horse trainer as well, having trained two tie-down horses of the year. Not too long ago, I was fortunate enough to have a conversation with Brent about his success. In our conversation, I asked Brent what he attributed his success to. His answer, "It's the mental game." He said, "The best thing that I had going for me in my career, and especially in 2000 when I won a lot, was that I was mentally prepared and had a really good attitude." Working hard and being mentally prepared that year resulted in Brent breaking the money earnings record at the time by winning $103,000 in just ten days. Placing in eight of the ten rounds and winning four of them led him to also win the average that same year. In our conversation, Brent went on to say that having a great mental game didn't just apply to rodeo. It applies to life.

This couldn't be truer. If there's one thing I've learned in recent years, it's that *how we think determines how we live*. In other words, if we want to be successful in life, especially when it comes to living for the Lord, we must have a strong mental game. I know what some of you are thinking, "Great, Beau's gone loco ... He's bought into this whole positive thinking mumbo jumbo." Not at all. Sadly, some misguided teachings about going to your happy place or thinking about butterflies and rainbows has led many followers of Christ to ignore the power of godly thinking. I'm not talking about thinking positive in place of God, I'm talking about positive thinking in response to who God is and what He can do.

I know for me, serving many hurting people, having the grind of message preparation, experiencing the exhaustion of delivering a message every Sunday, overseeing staff, etc. can really be overwhelming. And, although I'm not proud to admit it, sometimes I just want to quit. I find

The Mental Game

myself praying, "*Lord, I'm really not sure that I can do this much longer. Are you sure you still want me pastoring your church?*" It wasn't too long after this honest prayer that God answered me and said, "*Beau, I'm not ready for you to change what you do, I want you to change the way you think about what you do.*" This was so powerful for me to hear, because I knew that He'd called me to do what I was doing; I just had to learn to allow Him to change the way I thought about what I was doing! The truth is, how we think about our job, a negative experience, or our current relationship status can either lead us to live life to the fullest or lead to a life full of defeat and discouragement.

For me, instead of thinking, "Man, life stinks. So many are people hurting, so many marriages struggling, so many people are living without Christ, and I have to be in the middle of all of this." God wants me to change my thoughts to, "*Thank you Lord for allowing me to share your amazing healing and comfort with those who are hurting. Thank you for using me to give people hope in the midst of the hell they are experiencing.*" Or instead of thinking, "I can't stand studying. Having to type out this sermon every week is so hard." He wants me to change my thoughts and say to myself, "I get to read and study the greatest book ever written and share the greatest message ever told . . . what an honor and privilege."

Maybe for you it's the way you think about your

body or your past. Maybe you need to surrender those thoughts to Jesus and ask Him to teach you how to think godly thoughts about everything you face in life. This godly thinking is what has changed who I am and how I see life. And I'm telling you from my own personal experience, it works.

CHEW ON THIS
How do your thoughts affect your life? What current circumstance are you facing right now that is defeating you because you are thinking wrongly about what is happening to you? What scripture(s) can you use to fill your mind with the thoughts that give you life and honor God? Here are a few that come to mind for me: Colossians 3:1-2; Romans 12:1-2; Philippians 4:8.

PRAYER
Lord, I don't want to be defeated by my thoughts. I'm so sick and tired of losing the mental battle. Teach me how to think in a way that helps me live life to the fullest and bring you glory. Thank you for giving me the power to overcome anything I face in life.

DAY 9

Fight with a Texas Ranger

EPHESIANS 5:16
Make the most of every opportunity in these evil days. (NLT)

Nolan Ryan has to be my favorite baseball player of all time. He was a pitcher in the big leagues for twenty-seven years, playing the majority of those years with the Texas Rangers. He accrued 5,714 strikeouts, pitched seven no-hitters, and was inducted into the Baseball Hall of Fame in 1999. While it sounds like I'm a baseball fanatic, I'm not. The real reason I like Ryan is because he's a cattle rancher. He's been quoted saying, "Baseball allowed me to pursue my passion for ranching." And at the height of his cattle operation, he ran over 2,000 head.

Well, living in Oklahoma, if we wanted to watch an

The Maker's Mark

MLB game, we had to drive to Arlington, Texas to watch the Texas Rangers. We did this a lot over the years, but when it comes to Texas Rangers games there is one I'll never forget. It was the summer after my senior year of high school, and I'd been invited to tag along on a vacation to Texas with some friends of mine. I remember it like it was yesterday. While there, we were deciding what we wanted to do one night: go to a Texas Rangers baseball game or just go out to eat and hang at the hotel. Well, unfortunately we decided *not* to go to the Rangers game that night. I say "unfortunately" because, in the game that very night, Robin Ventura stormed the mound in an attempt to kick Ryan's a** after being drilled in the back by a pitch from Ryan. When Ventura got there, he was put in a headlock, where he received a face full of knuckle sandwiches from Ryan. I'll never forget seeing the replay of the fight and the pictures of Ryan back on the mound after the fight, with blood on his jersey. It was awesome! And I missed it!

Ever since that night, I've struggled with what the cool kids call *FOMO*. What's FOMO? It's the **F**ear **O**f **M**issing **O**ut. I hate it that I missed such a legendary moment, and to this day I don't want to miss another one like it.

When it comes to serving the Lord, I think a healthy dose of FOMO is a good thing. I say this because I feel like so many of us have become numb to the adventure

Fight with a Texas Ranger

and excitement of serving the Lord. We've become all too comfortable just going through the motions. Going from one Sunday to the next and calling it the Christian life while missing out on the supernatural experiences God wants us to have every day. I mean, where else can you have a front row seat to see someone change his or her destiny from hell to heaven by trusting in Jesus. Or maybe it's seeing a maverick teenager come back home because you chose to reach out to them. Maybe it's seeing a prayer answered when a friend of yours gets pregnant after the doctors said it was impossible! Or maybe it's rejoicing when one of your friends who was living a destructive lifestyle repents and turns back to Jesus. This is what life is all about, and we should desire to be present for every minute of it.

What I believe God wants for us is eyes to see the world the way He sees the world: in desperate need of a Savior. I believe that God wants us to take advantage of the opportunities that are right in front of us every day. There is always something exciting that God wants you to do. The question is: are you willing to do it? Are you prayed up and ready? Or are you settling for just sitting in the stands? It's time! It's time to step up onto the mound and take on our opponent, to fight for the souls of our friends, and to enjoy this exciting life we're called to live!

The Maker's Mark

CHEW ON THIS
What opportunities do you see right in front of you that God wants you to be a part of? When was the last time you saw God do a miracle in your life or someone else's because you took it upon yourself to do something? Where do you see God working right now and how can you join in the exciting things He's doing?

PRAYER
Jesus, I don't want to miss out on anything you have in store for me. Help me to see the world as you see it, and to not be afraid to dive in and get my hands dirty serving you. Thank you for this amazing opportunity to see lives changed for eternity.

DAY 10

Travelin' Partners

PROVERBS 13:20
Walk with the wise and become wise; associate with fools and get in trouble. (NLT)

Most rodeo athletes have people they travel with. Bronc riders typically travel with other bronc riders. Team ropers travel with their partners, bull riders with other bull riders. These buddies are often called travelin' partners. There are many benefits of traveling together as opposed to traveling by yourself. For instance, you have someone else to share the driving, you save money by sharing the cost of gas, and you have someone to help pull your rope or push your calf. Not to mention, if you go to the dance after the rodeo and ask a girl to dance who happens to have a jealous boyfriend you didn't know about, your boys are there to keep you alive if the boyfriend tries to beat the crap out of you! The most famous travelin' part-

The Maker's Mark

ners, that we've all probably heard of due to the movie *8 Seconds*, were Lane Frost, Tuff Hedemen, and Cody Lambert. These guys were the ultimate travelin' partners. They shared a smelly van, shared wins, shared getting beat up, shared dreams of being the best bull riders in the world, and, unfortunately, they shared the pain of losing a best friend.

Just like having travelin' partners while rodeoing is awesome, I believe that who we travel with on this ride called life makes all the difference in the world. Friends that love Jesus help us not give in when we get tired of doing what is right because we feel left out. Christ-centered travelin' partners help bring light to how the decisions we make today will affect us later on down the road. They encourage us and build us up spiritually. And when the devil attacks us, they're there to fight with us! I know for me, I wouldn't be half the man that I am today if it weren't for the men and women who I've had the pleasure of travelin' through life with. Men like my dad and father-in-law. Friends like Kreg Murphree, Josh Abbott, Ben Stewart, Jeremy Freeman, Chad Humphrey, and Mickey Bentley. My mentors: Billy Morgan, Ron Cline, Doug Melton, and Odus Compton. Women like my wife, Heather; my mom, Crickette; my friend, Cathy Whitaker, and many others. These outstanding people have traveled with me through thick and

Travelin' Partners

thin, and I'm forever grateful for their investment in me.

How about you? Do you have a list of Christ-centered travelin' partners that are shaping you to be more like Christ? If you don't, it's never too late to ask someone you admire and who has a growing relationship with Christ for some time together. Maybe it's just a twenty-minute conversation where you ask for wisdom on a decision. Maybe it's just calling them up and asking if you can ride in the pickup while they feed cows. Maybe it's pitching in to help them on a project at their house. It's in these life-on-life moments that God can transform you and grow you like never before. Maybe you have some great travelin' partners already. When was the last time you honored them for the difference they've made in your life? Don't wait, do it now.

CHEW ON THIS
Who in your life helps you become more like Christ? Or who's someone you've observed from afar who you know is growing in Christ that you'd like to build a friendship with? Maybe there's a friend that has encouraged you for years. Reach out to them today and let them know how thankful you are for them.

PRAYER
Jesus, show me who you want me to travel through this

The Maker's Mark

life with that will encourage me to be more like you. Help me to be that friend to others as well. And thank you for blessing me with the amazing Christ-centered friends that I already have.

DAY 11

Madeline's First Drive

ROMANS 12:11
Never be lazy, but work hard and serve the Lord enthusiastically. (NLT)

Not too long ago, I was invited to day-work with my good friend Marshall on the ranch he manages in West Texas. I've had the pleasure of day-working and photographing his brandings for many years, but this day was special because I was able to bring along my daughter Madeline. She was ten years old at the time, and this was the first time for her to make a big drive with some really great hands. We even got to stay in a bunkhouse on the ranch, which was pretty cool too. I'll never forget that morning as she mounted her ranch horse, Nacho, and we trotted

The Maker's Mark

out in line with the rest of the guys. It was still dark, the air was cool and moist, and the smell of rain was in the air. We were in a 2,600 acre pasture that ran beside a railroad, and at one point we were trotting next to the moving train like train robbers. It was very cool! As if that wasn't cool enough, after about a half mile of trotting in the dark, Madeline turned around with a big smile on her face and with excitement in her voice said, "This is awesome!"

I loved that moment, because I knew right then and there that she was getting to experience something that most kids, or adults for that matter, never get to experience. I mean, who can say that they've stayed in a bunkhouse on a big ranch, got up at 4:30 in the morning, set out in the dark with a great crew of cowboys and cowgirls, and got to be a part of gathering and working a big set of cows ... all before lunch? Not very many ten-year-olds I know can say that. It was awesome for me, too, because I love everything about cowboying, and getting to see the excitement and joy on my daughter's face made my heart happy.

Much like the experience that Madeline had that morning, I believe we can experience the same exhilarating rush when living for Christ. If we choose to, we can experience the joy of knowing that we get to do something exciting, something new, something supernatural each day we spend living for Him. Think about it: we get

Madeline's First Drive

to be a part of making a difference in eternity. We get to share with others how Jesus can wipe away their past. We get to feel the indescribable joy of seeing someone make a life-changing decision to follow Christ, going from spending eternity in a place of torment to spending an eternity in heaven. And if we're really blessed, we get to experience all of this with friends that are just as passionately living for Jesus.

Maybe as you're reading this, you realize that you've lost your passion for the Lord. Maybe you've grown numb to the miracles that God does around you every day. It's time to make a change! It's time to ask God to rekindle your fire for Him, to ask Him to make serving Him fresh and exciting again. I'd also suggest getting around some new believers that are on fire for the Lord, because the power of His grace is so fresh to them. Maybe you need to join a team at church so you can use your passion and gifts to serve the Lord and see first-hand the miracles He does so often. Like Madeline getting to ride and work with excitement, God wants us to serve Him with passion and enthusiasm and not settle for a mundane and meaningless life.

CHEW ON THIS

How's your passion for Christ? Have you lost it or is it still exciting to serve Him? Who in your life challenges you to

The Maker's Mark

be on fire for Christ? Choose today and every day to serve Jesus with joy and passion.

PRAYER
Lord, help me to serve you with excitement and joy. Surround me with people that love you and have a fire that hasn't gone out, so that I can burn bright for you too. Help others to see the thrill that I get from living for you and want to know that thrill as well.

DAY 12

Get Off on the Pain

1 TIMOTHY 6:17
Their trust should be in God, who richly gives us all we need for our enjoyment. (NLT)

I grew up in a family of wrestlers. Not steer wrestlers, just wrestlers. From the time I was seven years old to high school, we were a part of the sport of wrestling. If you aren't familiar with the sport, it's where two guys go head-to-head on a mat, trying to take each other to the mat and pin each other. It's rough, it's tough, and it's a great sport. Well, having two older brothers that knew a lot about wrestling and a lot about how to push my buttons meant that me getting taken down was a pretty common activity in our home. They would do whatever they could to antagonize me until we would tear into each other, and my mom would have to break us up or send us outside to have it out. For the record, and because

The Maker's Mark

I'm the author of this book, I just have to point out that I drew just as much blood out of them as they did out of me (they would say that's a bunch of crap, but it's true).

The toughness didn't stop with my brothers. My mom is one tough gal too. To this day, if I get smart with her, she will threaten and sometimes attempt to wrestle me to the ground, get her legs wrapped around me, and squeeze as hard as she can until I say "uncle." My dad on the other hand is a gentle, kindhearted man; he has that quiet toughness. He never raised his voice or got mad, but if you messed with him long enough, he would say things like, "Mess with the bull, you get the horns" or "Someone's going to end up crying." And he was usually right, because I either ended up crying or got frogged so hard I'd quit. This was just the way our family lived, and I liked it. From these experiences, I kind of learned to enjoy the pain. I know that sounds kinda sick, but it was fun.

While this mentality has probably helped me get through some pretty tough times in life, it's also led me, in some cases, to feel like I had to choose the hardest path possible to get to where God wanted me to be. I couldn't choose what I liked, I had to choose what was going to cause me to suffer a bit. I thought that if it wasn't painful or a major sacrifice, then it probably wasn't God's will. Looking back, I probably went through more challenges than I had to to get the same result God had in mind.

Get Off on the Pain

The truth we can take away from today's key verse is: doing God's will isn't always the hard thing to do. Sometimes it's the easiest thing to do and really enjoyable. For example, to serve the Lord, you don't have to leave everyone you know and move across the world or sell all your possessions. God may just be asking you to cross the street and invite your neighbor to church. His will may be to have a couple of friends over for dinner and enjoy a good time just hanging out, not an all-night prayer meeting. Maybe it's not that He's asking you to sacrifice a relationship with someone you've fallen in love with to please Him, but He wants you to get married and do life together, happily ever after. Maybe God isn't asking you to give up your dreams because He wants you to painfully endure a job you hate, maybe God's will is for you to live out your dreams by doing something you love. Sure, we have to embrace the suck sometimes because we live in an evil world where life is hard, pain is real, and some jobs aren't fun. But to always choose the path that is most painful isn't always God's will. Sometimes He just wants us to embrace His goodness, enjoy life, and give Him all the glory.

CHEW ON THIS
Are you going down a path of pain just because you're

The Maker's Mark

stubborn and think life has to be hard to please God? What pain are you going through that isn't God's will? What is something good that God has led you to do that you just need to embrace and enjoy?

PRAYER

God, I surrender my life to you. If you need me to suffer for your kingdom, I'm willing. But I also want to enjoy serving you, so help me to obey you and embrace your goodness.

DAY 13

Wasted

EPHESIANS 5:11
Take no part in the worthless deeds of evil and darkness; instead, expose them. (NLT)

When it comes to working with cattle, I've learned that some cows are easy to get along with no matter what happens. They don't get excited or snorty, they just go with the flow. But, on the other hand, I've also been around cattle that are easy-going until you put pressure on them. For instance, there are certain cows that usually leave you alone and don't try anything stupid as long as you leave them alone out in the pasture. But the moment you try to gather them or push them in a direction they don't want to go, they change into crazy winches. I've seen cows that are gone as soon as they see the trailer. Or they are looking for a place to escape the moment they step into the corral and you shut the gate. They may try jumping the fence, running you down, or just get so worked up that they fall down and refuse to get up.

We had a red Hereford like this that was respectfully named Reba (get it . . . Reba McEntire has red hair . . . red Hereford). Anyway, Reba was a great cow when it came to raising a big, healthy calf. But the moment you attempted to gather her or sort her out of the herd, she turned crazy. I can't tell you how many times we roped her and dragged her into the trailer. Or how many times, once we got her in the corral, she would try and jump out or hurt someone. She went crazy when you pressured her. Although this could be dangerous, if I am being honest, I sometimes enjoyed the excitement and challenge of trying to outsmart her. I just enjoy a good challenge every now and then. I like winning battles that seem impossible. To me, that's what makes life exciting!

The same can be said when it comes to our battle against evil. See, the devil is a lot like Reba. As long as you aren't a threat to him, he'll generally leave you alone. But the moment you decide to live out your faith, the fight is on. For example, the moment you start reading your Bible consistently is the moment you face a trial or temptation. Or the moment you start sharing your faith with your friends or expose a lie that they are tempted to believe is usually the moment you face persecution or discouragement. Unfortunately, after we experience

Wasted

his attacks a few times, many of us second-guess living for Jesus. We tend to want to shrink back and not stand out. We keep to ourselves and try to just keep our head down and do life. Why? Because no sane person enjoys being attacked or beat up. We want life to be fun, not filled with battles and hardships. Don't get me wrong, it can suck to do what's unpopular or counter-cultural, but we have to remember that this is what it means to love and serve Jesus.

Jesus actually promises that we will face bad stuff when we live for Him. In John 16:33 He says, "I have told you all this so that you may have peace in me. Here on earth you will have many trials and sorrows. But take heart, because I have overcome the world" (NLT). Notice He didn't say, "You *might* have trials," but, "you *will* have trials." While this doesn't sound fun, what we must realize is that the easy, comfortable, no-threat-to-the-enemy way of life is really a wasted life. A life that doesn't leave a legacy of battles that we fought and won, a life that never enters the arena but stays in the stands isn't really a life worth living. We've been called to fight the good fight, to take ground for Jesus, to fight for the souls of man. We've been called to live a life on the offense, taking back what the devil hijacks, not just living in comfort and ease. Christ has asked us to enter the dark places of this world and shine bright for Him. Is it easy? Heck no! But is worth it? Always! When we live in such a way that causes the devil to feel threatened or scared, we can go to bed at night, no matter what circumstances we're in, knowing that we are making a difference. So, don't waste your life not living for Christ because you're afraid of the devil's attack. Know that a life lived for Christ is always worth the fight, and you have the greatest warrior fighting with you—His name is Jesus.

CHEW ON THIS

Are you a threat to the devil? Or are you just living a comfortable life because you don't want anything bad to happen to you or your family? It's time to count the cost and get back into the fight. Commit today to becoming a threat to the devil by living out your faith and making an eternal difference in this world.

PRAYER

Lord, I want to make a difference for you. Help me not to fear the attack of the devil but to live for you no matter the cost. Strengthen me for the fight and give me victory over my enemy, the devil.

DAY 14

Open Another Gate

1 CORINTHIANS 9:22
To the weak I became weak, to win the weak. I have become all things to all people so that by all possible means I might save some.

I've used my truck and a sack of cake many times to get my cattle in the pens. So, not too long ago I set out to do just that. I pulled up, the cows saw my truck and came running. I got out, poured the cake into the feed bunks, and the cows rolled right through the gate and into the corrals. What was different about this day was that I needed to load all my cows and move them to a different pasture. So after successfully getting them caught, I backed my trailer up to the gate and began loading them.

The Maker's Mark

After getting about half of them loaded in the front of the trailer, I shut the middle gate and was headed back to load the rest of them. When I stepped out of the trailer, I spooked one of the calves that was still in the corrals, and she ran through the corral fence and got out on the road. Scared, she quickly turned and began to trot down the blacktop. I jumped the fence, got on the other side of the road, snuck around her, and began to try and push her back towards the corrals. To my relief, as I was doing this, she decided to climb back through the pasture fence into our place. I know what you're thinking, "Hey Beau, sounds like you need some better fences," to which I'd say, "I know, Mr. Obvious."

While getting her back through the fence was good because she was back in our pasture, I now had to figure out how to get her back into the corrals so I could get her loaded. If you've ever gathered cattle and gotten them in the pens only for them to get right back out, you know how hard it is to get them to go back into the corrals right after they've escaped. While I knew that her momma and the rest of the cows would draw her back to the trailer, I also knew that it would be a miracle to get her to go back through the same gate she went through before. But being the stubborn man that I am, I went ahead and tried. After thirty minutes of waiting and then attempting to push her, and even letting a few of the cows out

Open Another Gate

of the trailer back into the corrals to try and draw her through the same gate, I gave up—it wasn't working. So, finally I did what I should have done from the beginning: I shut the gate she had gone through the first time and opened the panels on the other end of the corrals, giving her a new option to get in. I then got around her and, ever so gently, nudged her down the fence toward that new opening, and she trotted right in.

I've served in church leadership for over two decades now. One of the things I've noticed, is that churches who are willing to change *how* they do church—willing to try new things and not hold on too tightly to the-way-we've-always-done-things mentality—those churches reach the most people. These churches understand that the way we've reached people in the past isn't always going to work to reach them in the future. Just like I had to find a new way to get that calf into the pen, wise churches must be willing to change the methods they use to reach those who don't know Christ.

What we have to realize is that the world is changing all the time, and, though we will never change the unchanging message of Jesus and the power of His Word, we must be willing to change the method in which we deliver it. Maybe you're a leader in the church. Maybe you serve on a team at church. Don't be afraid to change something up. Don't be afraid to open a new gate so that more people can come to know Christ.

CHEW ON THIS
What do you see that needs to change in your church so that you can reach more people for Christ? What can you do to support and encourage your pastors to help them change how your church reaches the world? What can you do personally to make that change happen?

PRAYER
Lord, as much as it depends on me, help me to always be willing to change to reach whoever you have for me to reach. Help my church to always be willing to do things that no one else is doing to reach people that no one else is reaching.

DAY 15

Can You Still Rope?

2 CORINTHIANS 4:17
For our light and momentary troubles are achieving for us an eternal glory that far outweighs them all.

Not too long ago, some friends of mine and I entered a ranch rodeo in Vernon, Texas. We had been day-working together quite a bit and felt like it would be fun to go show our skills in the arena. Or maybe we just thought we'd donate our money to the cause like we normally did! A few events into the rodeo, things were going well, and we had a time in every event. Then it came time for the branding event. For some reason, the guys asked me to rope, so I said, "sure, I'll give it a whirl." If you've never been to a ranch rodeo, it's not like your normal rodeo. The events portray the everyday jobs you might see on the ranch minus the wild cow milking. It's just for the crowd. Things like doctoring cattle, gathering strays, and

The Maker's Mark

penning cattle are things cowboys do on the ranch. The branding event is also just like what you'd see on the ranch, except in the rodeo you're competing against the clock and twenty other teams for the fastest time. Two four-man teams go at a time and, when the flag drops, one person from each team rides into a pen of calves and tries to rope a calf by its two hind feet and drag it to the guys on the ground to be branded with chalk. Once the team has branded two calves, the time stops. At this particular rodeo the teams were separated by panels, and, because I wasn't always confident that I could get my dally, I tied on to my saddle horn.

The time started, I rode in, roped the first calf, and brought him out. The boys branded him, and we let him back into the herd. I then went back and roped the next calf, which was a pretty good size, and when I turned to ride out of the pen, I let the rope slide through my hand until the rope came tight. But, for some reason, this time a coil got wrapped around my middle three fingers, ripping off my middle finger nail. I'm not sure how it didn't take the other two finger nails, but I'm sure glad it didn't. Looking down at my hand, I quickly realized that I needed to get something on my finger, or it was just going to bleed all over everything. After showing the guys what just happened, and because they are known for having great compassion, they replied, "Can you still rope?" To

Can You Still Rope?

which I replied, "you're dang right I can." We found a leather glove, I put it on, and we finished the rodeo.

Truth is, sometimes as Christians we have to play hurt. What do I mean? Let me explain. Just like I had to finish the rodeo that night even though I was hurt, as followers of Christ we are called to live for Him even when we're hurt. Sure, God gives us time to heal eventually, but sometimes we just have to grit our teeth, bear down, and suck it up. While everyone goes through pain and hurt, I believe that pastors face more hurt than most people ever dream of. Unless you've ever been a pastor, you have no clue what your pastor goes through. I've heard people say things like, "Well, if I were the pastor, I'd ... blah, blah, blah ..." It takes everything inside of me not to stop them and say, "You're not a pastor, so don't even talk." I don't mean to sound harsh, but it's just true. Let me give you some facts about pastors: Pastors take more heat than cheers. We're always in a fight with the devil. Preaching a sermon is like giving birth on Sunday, and finding out you're pregnant on Monday. The labor never ends and the delivery is exhausting. Most pastors are lonely and don't have a trusted friend. More often than not, pastors do their job hurt. The struggle of marriage and having kids is one thing. But then add the fish bowl that we live in, the expectations of others, and the pain and struggles of everyone you pastor. This takes hurt to a whole other level. Again, I'm not saying that people with other jobs don't struggle or get hurt, because they do. But I know personally the hurt that comes with pastoring people.

I'd encourage you to follow the teaching in Hebrews 13:17, which says, "Have confidence in your leaders and submit to their authority, because they keep watch over you as those who must give an account. Do this so that their work will be a joy, not a burden, for that would be of no benefit to you." This verse tells us not to be the cause of our spiritual leaders' burdens, but the cause of their joy. That way, your pastor can fulfill his calling and stay healthy, not hurt.

You too may be facing some pain or disappointment in your life today. Maybe you've been hurt by someone at work, betrayed by a family member, or even been hurt by someone in the church. Maybe your pain is something that you are enduring physically because of illness or disease. Know that you're not alone. God is with you and He will get you through the pain. Know also that sometimes you just have to suck it up, not lose faith, and finish the race that God has you in. Living for Christ isn't pain-free, but if we are faithful and stay hooked, we will reap the rewards if we do not give up.

By the way, we didn't win the rodeo in Vernon, but we did finish it. I didn't take that glove off until I got home at about 1:00 a.m., and my wife had to cut the glove off

Can You Still Rope?

of my hand because it was full of dry blood. Good times!

CHEW ON THIS
Where are you hurting today? What is one thing that you know you can do to keep moving forward in spite of the pain? What job do you need to finish even though it's painful? Turn to God now and don't give up.

PRAYER
Lord, I want to give up. But I'm not going to. I just ask that you would give me the hope and strength that I need to get through this season of pain. I trust you with life and know that you are right beside me through it all.

DAY 16

The Birds and the Bulls

GENESIS 2:25
Now the man and his wife were both naked, but they felt no shame. (NLT)

As a pastor, I've taught about God's design for sex for years. Whether it was as a student pastor or as a senior pastor, I made teaching on the gift of sex a part of many series—series like "Victorious Secret: Biblical Secrets for Finding Victory in Dating, Marriage, and Sex," "Riding Double," "Sittin' in a Tree," and "Going All the Way." I love teaching on the subject. While I have no problem standing in front of a group of people and sharing what God says about sex, it was a different story when it came to having "the talk" with my ten-year-old son, Hank. For

The Birds and the Bulls

a few months or so, he had been asking questions. He'd hear the word on TV, at school, and even in church, so inevitably he would throw out questions about it. Like, "What is sex? What is sexy?" He even showed me a sexual gesture that one of his classmates made and he wanted to know what it meant, to which I responded, "I'll tell you later." After dropping his head in disappointment, he replied, "Dad, you sure have a lot to tell me later." It wasn't long after that that I felt God telling me it was time to start the conversation.

So, like every good father, I sat him down and began by saying, "You know how sometimes when we're in the pasture the bull jumps on a cow's back and rides the cow?" Hank nodded his head yes. I continued, "Well buddy, that's sex. And that's how cows get pregnant" (don't judge me . . . you work with what you know, and I'll work with what I know). I went on to tell him that, as humans, God gave us the gift of sex as well. I shared that it takes two people, a man and a woman, to have a baby, and that sex is one of the greatest gifts God gave couples to enjoy in marriage. He then asked, "So, do you and mom have sex?" To which I replied, "Yes, we do. Because we're married, mommy and daddy get to enjoy having sex together. So, when mommy and daddy's bedroom door is locked, that usually means we are 'worshipping'" (our code word for having sex). Hank then replied, "Well, your door's not locked that much," to which I burst out laughing and said, "You're right son, you're so right. It's not locked nearly enough."

Now that I've had "the birds and the bulls" talk with Hank, I'm so grateful that he came to me with his questions. We must understand that this is not the time to be silent but to speak truth into our children's lives. Fact is: what we avoid, the devil invades; therefore, we must speak into their lives, because, if we don't, the devil most definitely will. Remember, God has given us all the answers we need in His Word, and as Christian parents it's our privilege and honor to teach our kids God's perfect plan for sex. What's cool about God is that from creation—starting with Adam and Eve, who were both naked and felt no shame—He has given sex to us for our enjoyment and His glory. All joking aside, I do believe that God sees sex in marriage as an act of worship, and He rejoices when we partake of this blessing.

If you're a parent and you're anxious, like I was, to talk to your kids about sex, don't be. When God reveals that it's the appropriate time, go for it. Be positive, use scripture, and set your kids up for sexual holiness and purity. If you're a pre-teen and your parents haven't had the birds and bulls talk with you and you're reading this . . . well . . . sorry, not sorry! At least now you know what God says about sex, and I pray that you will commit to

The Birds and the Bulls

live according to His design for sex. If you have more questions about sex, but your parents aren't Christians and you don't think their advice would be the best, I'd encourage you to go to your student pastor or senior pastor and ask them. If you're a college student or a single adult and you have questions about who to date, how to stay sexually pure, or how to know if the person you're dating is the right one, I'd encourage you to also go and ask a trusted Christian mentor or pastor. There are also some really great books out there for young singles that can help guide you, like *The Right One* by Jimmy Evans. There are also some great podcasts led by some really wise believers to help set you up for success. Do whatever it takes to get the right answers about sexuality, marriage, and dating.

CHEW ON THIS

Parents: what are you doing to intentionally set your kids up for success when it comes to sex?

Students: who are you asking advice from? Your parents? Christ-centered friends and mentors? Or friends that aren't walking with Christ?

Young adults: what commitments and boundaries are you living by now to honor God with your sexuality?

The Maker's Mark

PRAYER

Prayer for parents: *Lord, I want to set my kids up to honor you when it comes to their sexuality. Give me the wisdom and answers that please you and align with your Word.*

Prayer for students and young adults: *I want to walk in purity and honor you and my future spouse with my body. Show me how to live, so I can remain sexually pure and holy.*

DAY 17

The Birds and the Bulls: Part 2

1 THESSALONIANS 4:3-5
God's will is for you to be holy, so stay away from all sexual sin. Then each of you will control his own body and live in holiness and honor—not in lustful passion like the pagans who do not know God and his ways. (NLT)

I hate waiting. For instance, when it comes to feeding cattle, I hate waiting for all the cows to come in before I put out the feed. I think, "if you aren't fast enough to get here before it's all gone, then you don't deserve to eat." But, as you probably know, it's worth waiting on all of them to get there, that way they all get the same amount of nutrients. I also hate waiting for my cows to go through the gate. I don't want to wait; I want to try and push them through, but that never goes well. Am I the only one like this? I doubt it. What I learn time and time again is that, contrary to my impatient nature, it's always worth it to wait.

The same can be said when it comes to saving the gift of sex for marriage. Although it's contrary to our natural desire and although it's counter to pop culture, waiting for marriage to have sex is always worth the wait. I know what some of you are thinking, "Man, Beau, that's hard," and you're right. Speaking from a male perspective, when we become teenagers, our sex drive kicks in. We naturally think about sex all the time. We sometimes can't even find relief when we're sleeping because we even have dreams about sex. Our desire for sex is so strong that sometimes it's overwhelming. Trust me, I understand. But let me tell you from a man who, by the grace of God, made it to his wedding day a virgin: it's all worth the wait! It's worth the lonely nights. It's worth the dateless years. It's worth it! It's worth not dating that hot girl who's not a Christian. It's worth not going to the parties where you know you'll be tempted. It's worth it!

Don't get me wrong . . . I wasn't perfect and I did things while dating that I regret, but I always kept my pants on. The truth is: the sacrifice, the battles with temptation, even the humiliation from others are all worth going through when you reach your honeymoon night able to give your spouse such a precious gift.

The Birds and the Bulls: Part 2

Sadly, many people have only heard the reasons not to have sex: "You'll get an STD, you might get pregnant, you'll ruin your Christian reputation," while never hearing the blessings of waiting. Let me share a few: I have no one to compare sex with my wife to; she doesn't have to worry if I'm thinking about a past sexual experience with another girl; I don't have any sexual baggage or scars; when my kids ask me if I waited until marriage to have sex, I'm able to say, "yes sweetie, I did." I can keep going . . . I have no shame or regret. These are just a few of the rewards for waiting, and, though I had to practice self-control for what was realistically a short period, I now get to enjoy a lifetime of sexual enjoyment and freedom with my wife. By the way, my wife, Heather, was also a virgin when we married, and she was able to receive all of these blessings as well.

Did I mention that I was twenty-eight years old and my wife was twenty-two when we had sex for the first time? Some would say, "If I have to wait that long, I'll never make it." Well, I can honestly say that I would have never made it to marriage without the grace of God and the community I had around me. First off, I was challenged by my pastors to make a public commitment to save sex for marriage, which gave me much needed accountability. I had parents who I know hit their knees every time I went on a date, asking God to keep me pure.

The Maker's Mark

As a student pastor myself, I had young people looking to me for leadership on how to live for Christ. I only dated girls who loved Jesus and wanted to honor Him, and I set boundaries with the girls I dated and communicated those before the physical temptations were there. Because I had surrendered my life to Jesus, I had the Holy Spirit living inside of me to protect, guide, and convict me when I needed it. Was it easy? Heck no! Even with all of those guardrails, I can't tell you how many times I had sexual thoughts, lusted, and came close to crossing the line. It was a battle. But what I can tell you now is that the rewards are worth the fight.

Maybe you're a teenager or a young single guy or gal and you're facing sexual temptations. Do whatever it takes to stay holy. Make a commitment to God and to others to live in sexual purity. Set boundaries before you are tempted. Get rid of apps on your phone that tempt you to think sexually impure thoughts.

CHEW ON THIS

Have you committed to saving sex for marriage? Why or why not? Are you struggling to remain sexually pure? Have you made your commitment to sexual purity public with a trusted friend so they can help hold you accountable? Are you dating Christ-centered people? Are you

The Birds and the Bulls: Part 2

plugged into a church community that can help you stay strong in this sex-crazed world?

PRAYER

Lord, I want to honor you with my body and my sexuality. Empower me to stay away from sexual sin. Give me supernatural control over my sexual desires. Grant me the wisdom to know what tempts me and the strength to overcome those temptations. Thank you that, through your power and the help of godly friends, I can remain holy and pure for your glory and my good.

DAY 18

Tied On Green

ROMANS 12:3
Don't think you are better than you really are. Be honest in your evaluation of yourselves, measuring yourselves by the faith God has given us. (NLT)

I had only been cowboying a few months when a friend of mine asked me to come help work his calves. Thinking I was all that and a bag of chips, I said, "sure, I'll come help." So, the morning came and we had gathered all the cows, sorted off the mommas, and were ready to drag. There were only about five or six people helping, so we decided to use some Nordforks so that we could have more people roping and giving shots. One of the guys helping that morning was an older gentleman named Gary. He was a great hand and rode really nice horses. On this particular day, he was riding a pretty little red-roan horse that was

Tied On Green

all sorts of fancy.

Ready to get started, my friend asked Gary and me if we'd both like to start out dragging. Having two people roping in the pen at the same time was something that I'd never done before, but I didn't think twice when I tied on and proceeded to go rope a calf. Even though the pen was a little small, Gary and I were able to rope at the same time and drag calves to the Nordforks. It wasn't too long into the morning when Gary rode in beside me, threw his loop at an un-worked calf, and missed. Turning his horse as if to ride out of the pen, Gary stopped his horse and proceeded to gather his rope while paying no attention to me. Thinking nothing about it, I threw my loop, quickly catching two hind feet. But this time was different, because I was too close to Gary and had too much slack in my rope. The slack allowed the calf to scramble behind Gary's horse; I couldn't get my rope off the saddle horn in time and my rope ran just over Gary's horse's hocks, burning them and causing Gary's horse to buck him off.

Immediately realizing that this was not good situation, I rode forward, jerked my rope off the saddle-horn, and jumped off to see if Gary was alright. Being the tough gentleman that he was and after catching his breath, Gary made it to his feet and seemed to be fine. We ended up finishing the work, but man did I feel bad about what happened. After that, I realized that I had no business being

The Maker's Mark

tied on in the branding pen with anyone. I had clearly overestimated my skills and I nearly got someone hurt.

Maybe I'm the only one, but I've often found myself riding the line between being confident and being conceited. For instance, I want my words and actions to show that I have confidence in God, but they often come across boastful. I want my talents and gifts to bring God glory, but it often seems like I'm trying to take credit for my success. What I learn a little bit more and more every day is that pride or conceit never take you where you think they will. Thinking too highly of your talents never makes you better at something. It actually sets you up to be humiliated when you fall short of what you claimed you were good at. (By the way, being prideful or conceited can be something that we deal with internally and doesn't have to be spoken to be wrong. A person can be conceited and never say a word.)

Conceit also never satisfies your deepest need for approval. It never earns you the respect you think you deserve and it never results in true friendships. What it does result in is more insecurity because you're relying on your own assessment to find your worth. Instead of gaining respect from others, it actually causes them to lose respect for you. Instead of attracting others, it actually repels them. But confidence, or Godfidence, on the other hand, is found in knowing who God has made you to be and finding your security and worth in Him. Today's key verse tells us to "not think you are better than you really are . . . measuring yourselves by the faith God has given you." This verse tells us that we are to measure ourselves by the faith that God has given us. A faith that we didn't earn or create, a faith that is given to us from God. Therefore, our talents, skills, and experiences are all gifts from Him, and He's the one who gets the praise. Don't be like me and have to learn the hard way that conceit doesn't pay.

CHEW ON THIS
Which side of the line do you fall? Godfidence or being conceited? Is there a story in your life where God had to humble you to bring you back to reality? Share it with someone today.

PRAYER
Lord, help me to view all of my talents and abilities as gifts from you. Thank you for the experiences and talents that I do have—use them to bring you glory and honor!

DAY 19

Using Gear

EPHESIANS 2:10
For we are his workmanship, created in Christ Jesus for good works, which God prepared beforehand, that we should walk in them. (ESV)

As I mentioned on Day 1, Billy Klapper is famous for making really great cowboy gear. From the working cowboys who've saved up their money for years just to purchase a set of Klapper spurs, to some of the greatest horse trainers in the world, Klapper gear is highly sought after. Nowa-days, a pair of Klapper spurs may take a year to get, and the base price starts at $2,100. Although I've never owned a Klapper bit or set of spurs myself, I know people who do, and, in their words, there is no comparison. The feel, the way a horse carries the bit, and the response you get from a Klapper bit is special.

According to Mr. Klapper's friends and clients, there's

Using Gear

one thing he expects from all his customers. He wants them to *use his gear*. One of my good friends, who happens to own a few Klapper bits, told me that Mr. Klapper is even leery of making any spurs or bits without the customer's initials or brand on the piece, because he doesn't want it to be sold online to a collector who'll never use it.

When I heard this, I couldn't help but think that God probably views us the same way. Just like Mr. Klapper wants his gear to be used, God has created us to be used. Sadly, like those collectors who buy Klapper's work just to put them on a shelf or sell on eBay, many Christians place themselves on a spiritual shelf, never to be used by God. Sure, they may attend church when it's convenient or sing a few words of the worship songs, but they don't actually get out of their comfort zone and allow God to work through them. Tragically, this is far too common.

I have a great friend named Mickey that I fondly refer to as my "mangy" friend. I say that jokingly, but he does chase coyotes, so he's bound to have had a little mange on him at some point. I first met Mickey and his family when I took a job as the student minister at the church they attended. Because we shared a lot of the same passions like hunting, horses, and cattle, we hit it off. He and his family quickly became like family to me, and we've shared lots of great times ever since. When we met, Mickey was just a good Sunday church-going kinda guy,

The Maker's Mark

and that was it. If you asked him to do much else, he was out. Well, somehow I talked Mickey into going to summer camp with our students as a sponsor. And, as Mickey tells the story, it was during one night at camp that, for first time in his life, he heard the Holy Spirit speak to him. Prompted by God to ask a kid named Chance if he had ever been saved, Mickey was able to share Jesus' love with him and led Chance to Christ that very night. I believe that night not only changed Chance's life for eternity, but Mickey's life too. From that point on, Mickey began looking for ways to be used by God. He became a person that loved sharing his faith with others; he started leading Bible studies at church and leading his family to grow in their faith—all because he obeyed the prompting of the Holy Spirit and allowed God to use him.

The point is this: God created you and me to be used. We weren't created to just go to work, come home, and sit in our easy chair. We are called to be bold in our love for others—and to serve others—all in the name of Jesus. So, the question is: are you letting God use you? Or are you just blending in, going with the flow, not wanting to stand out because of your faith? Just like Mr. Klapper desires for his gear to be used, God wants to use you to make a difference in this world.

Using Gear

CHEW ON THIS

Are you just cruising through life, not really making an eternal difference? When was the last time you allowed God to work through you? What was the result? What step do you need to take today to begin allowing God to use you?

PRAYER

Lord Jesus, I want to be used by you. I don't want to just be a casual Christian. I want to be all in. So, I'm asking you to use me today and every day to make a difference in eternity.

DAY 20

Dead or Alive

2 CORINTHIANS 10:4
We use God's mighty weapons, not worldly weapons, to knock down the strongholds of human reasoning and to destroy false arguments. (NLT)

As I mentioned earlier, we used to own a red Hereford cow named Reba that was crazy. At the time, I had about forty pairs, including Reba and her calf, on a pasture that wasn't the best pasture for wild cattle. It was part wheat pasture, but the rest was overrun with cedar trees. Finding wild cattle in cedars can be almost impossible. After running my cows there all summer, my lease was up and we needed to gather them and get them off. Just like all the other times we gathered them before, Reba wasn't going to be caught very easily. As soon as she saw the trailer, her head went up and she ran through the fence

Dead or Alive

and into the cedars. We got everything gathered but her.

So, a few days later, me and my buddies Jason and Justin set out horseback with some dogs to try and gather her. It was impossible. Reba would see us from a mile away and make it to the cedars before we could get a rope on her. She even outran the dogs. We tried catching her for weeks, and we never did. Not too long after that, she went missing. Every time I would go out to see if I could catch her on the wheat, she was nowhere to be found. I went to all the neighbors asking if they'd seen her . . . nothing. Winter came, snow fell, and no one saw her for almost a year, so I wrote her off as dead.

Until one day, I got a call from a neighbor who had taken over the lease and had been running some yearlings on the same pasture. He said, "Hey man, I've got one of your cows caught in a trap with my cows. Do you want to come get her?" To which I replied, "I don't have any cows there anymore, so she can't be mine." To which he responded, "I'm sure she's yours. She's a red cow with your brand on her and has an ear tag with your phone number on it." *A red cow? A Hereford? No way!* I thought to myself, *after all this time . . . could it be Reba?* I hung up the phone, hooked onto my trailer, and headed over to his place as fast as I could. When I got there, to my astonishment, there she stood. Reba. In all her crazy glory! When I told my neighbor how wild she was, he replied, "She just came right in with the others, no problem." I looked at him and thought to myself, *you're one heck of a hand to get that done.* He did something that, even with help from my buddies, I couldn't get done. I loaded Reba up and took her straight to the sale barn, never to see her again!

Just like Reba, I think all of us have things in our lives that we've written off as dead, only to have them show up again—a lie that eats at us once again, an addiction that creeps back up, or a habit that becomes tempting again. We've tried lots of times to overcome it, we've even asked for help, only for it to go away for a little while but then return again. What I've learned in life is that there is only one name that every temptation, every addiction, every thought, every sin has to bow to . . . it's the name of Jesus. And just like my neighbor easily did what I wasn't able to do, Jesus can overcome anything with the same ease because He is the all-powerful Savior of the world! He is our hope, our strength, our shield, and our greatest weapon against sin.

CHEW ON THIS

What sinful habit, temptation, or thought tends to show up in your life after you thought it was dead? What do you find yourself faced with time and time again that you need Jesus to overcome? Hand it over to Him and let Him demolish it once and for all.

PRAYER

Jesus, I need you to overcome the temptations I'm facing today. Rid me of the wrong thoughts, actions, and sinful habits in my life once and for all.

DAY 21

Double-Wide Blessing

JOSHUA 1:8

Keep this Book of the Law always on your lips; meditate on it day and night, so that you may be careful to do everything written in it. Then you will be prosperous and successful.

Though I've been blessed to ride on some really great ranches in my life, I didn't grow up on a big ranch. From the time I was in elementary school through junior high, I grew up on a five-acre spread in Mustang, Oklahoma. Though it was a small piece of land, I had everything a kid could want. My family lived in a trailer house that wasn't just a single-wide, it was a double-wide. That's right, a double-wide! We had an above ground pool with a deck on one side where my brothers and I would play King of

Double-Wide Blessing

the Deck. As you can imagine, this game ultimately led to someone slipping on the wet wood and busting something open. We had a pond. We had neighborhood kids to play with (or get in fights with, depending on the day). We had a huge garden that, for some reason, was really good at growing okra. To this day, I can't stand okra because all I remember was how bad it hurt my hands to pick it. But that garden fed us for years. After my dad went to the Oklahoma City stockyards and bought one hundred baby chicks, we had plenty of fried chicken and eggs. We had so many eggs we sold them to the neighbors for a dollar a dozen. On top of all that, my dad made friends with a guy that worked for Kellogg's, and this guy would give us all the "slightly" out-of-date cereal we could eat (don't judge my parents, they had three hungry boys to feed, so free was always the right price). We had Captain Crunch with berries, Cookie Crisp, Rice Krispies, and Frosted Flakes. We even had Grape Nuts, which was my dad's favorite. We also had goats, rabbits, snakes, and horned toads (a.k.a. horny toads).

The greatest blessing of all was, while living there, I got my first horse and saddle. I think the saddle cost more than the horse, but I didn't care. You may be thinking, "You're kind of proud of such a small place." To which I'd say, "You're dang right I am!" We had everything we needed and more.

The Maker's Mark

Thinking about it now, I can't help but wonder why we were so blessed? But then I was reminded of today's key verse: "Keep this Book of the Law always on your lips; meditate on it day and night, so that you may be careful to do everything written in it. Then you will be prosperous and successful" (Joshua 1:8). This verse tells us that if we will live by God's Word, we will succeed and prosper. My dad calls this verse the "key to success," and I believe that we were so blessed because my parents took God at His word and lived by the truths found in Bible.

It was because my mom wasn't afraid to share her faith with anyone who would listen, and even some who didn't want to listen, that God's favor was on us. It was because my dad woke up every morning—drank raw eggs, milk, and honey (like Rocky)—then turned the weather channel on mute, sat down in his recliner, and read God's Word. We were blessed because almost every night we would kneel at my parent's bed and pray together. It was because my parents made sure we blessed every meal and went to church every time the doors were opened. It was because they did their best to obey God and live for His glory, that we had all our needs met. Don't misunderstand what I'm saying here. It wasn't *for* God's approval or love that my parents lived for Him. It was *in response to* His love and forgiveness that they led us in living for His glory, and God happily fulfilled His promise to provide for us.

For some of you, up until this point you've lived your life by your own set of rules and desires. You've made decisions based only on what you wanted and what you thought would make you happy. And, for some of you, this has only led to one failure after another. What you thought would bring success hasn't. I want to encourage you today to stop living according to your own ways and turn to God's Word to show you how to truly live. I can promise you that it will lead to favor and blessing on your life. I'm not saying you'll get rich and have a fancy house and rig, but I can promise that God will meet your every need. And, because He's so cool, He often tends to not only meet your needs but give you some of your wants as well.

You may be on the other end of the scale, and in the world's eyes your life looks like a success. You own a big ranch, with nice fancy barns, and have cows all over the place, but for some reason you find no lasting fulfillment in these things. I would also encourage you to turn to God's Word, learn His plan and will for your life, and begin to live for Him. I can promise you that you will find no greater fulfillment than what you do in Jesus' name. And remember, blessing is blessing. It doesn't matter how many square-feet your house is. It doesn't matter how many acres you have. It doesn't matter if you get to eat fresh cereal or out-of-date cereal . . . blessing is blessing. And blessings come from following Jesus.

CHEW ON THIS
Are you living by God's Word or following your own plan? In what area of your life do you need to become more obedient to Christ so that you can receive all that God has for you? When was the last time you thanked God for what you have?

PRAYER
God, I thank you for the blessings that I have. If there is any area of my life that's not pleasing to you, reveal it to me so that I can receive all that you have for me and live my life for your pleasure and not my own.

DAY 22

Shrink

HEBREWS 10:39
But we do not belong to those who shrink back and are destroyed, but to those who have faith and are saved.

My friend Merle was the first person to teach me the impact of shrink. We'd brought his weaned calves to the sale so that they could be sold a few days later. After the cattle were unloaded and settled in their pens, Merle and I went out back to check on them. When we got to the pens, I noticed that Merle went into every pen, cleaned out the water trough, and shuffled the feed around in the feed bunk. Later, when I asked him why he did this, he shared with me that he did it to make sure that his cattle had access to plenty of fresh water and fresh feed. Why? Because he wanted them to drink and eat as much as they could before they were sold. See, he knew the effects shrink had on the price of his cattle.

The Maker's Mark

Some of you may be lost and wondering what the heck shrink is. Well, it's just what it sounds like. It's when cattle experience weight or muscle loss (shrinkage), thereby, affecting the seller's bottom dollar. While shrink can be caused by a number of things, generally it results from the stress cattle experience while being handled, processed, or transported. I could bore you with a lot of facts and numbers, but I'll just share a few. Just the act of weighing cattle can cause shrinkage. Cattle can also shrink while being transported long distances. So, the question becomes: how do we prevent this from happening? The short answer is, you reduce the stress put on cattle, and the second answer to the question is what Merle taught me. You have to get them back on feed and water as quickly as possible.

Much like cattle that are being marketed, we live in a society that is filled with anxiety and stress. Especially among millennials, stress and anxiety are at an all-time high. While millennials are the most tech-savvy generation in human history, they are the most anxious as well. You may be thinking, "This is a town kid issue. This doesn't affect kids that grow up on the ranch or in small towns." If you think this, you would be mistaken. Every young cowboy I ride with has a cell phone. And when their hands are free, they're on it—checking their feed on the gram and wondering what they're missing out on.

Shrink

Studies are showing that, because of technology, millennials are being given so many choices, and changes are happening every second, thereby leading these young adults to stress over keeping up. The *swipe-right generation*, as they're known, are more worried about the future than any other generation before them.

Because of the stress and anxiety plaguing our culture today, many Christians, of all ages, are experiencing what I'd call *spiritual shrink*. In other words, because of the stress of life, many believers are not growing in their faith. They've gone away from feeding on God's Word, and are paralyzed by fear. We've lost sight of the power that we have in Christ to not be overcome by the world. We've given into the rapid pace of the world and lost sight of what really matters. And in many ways, we've lost our spiritual boldness. We avoid situations that would cause us to live counter to the culture, causing even more spiritual shrink in our lives.

What's the answer? Well, when I don't know what to do, I always do what I know . . . and I know that God's Word never fails. And just like cattle need feed and water to regain the weight they've lost due to shrink, God's Word, also known as the bread of life, can help us to regain our spiritual weight. Our key verse is a part of a chapter in scripture that I believe gives us the answer and hope that we need today. Listen to Paul, the writer of the book of Hebrews, as he sounds the call for the church to persevere and not shrink back:

> So do not throw away your confidence; it will be richly rewarded. You need to persevere so that when you have done the will of God, you will receive what he has promised. For, "In just a little while, he who is coming will come and will not delay." And, "But my righteous one will live by faith. And I take no pleasure in the one who shrinks back." But we do not belong to those who shrink back and are destroyed, but to those who have faith and are saved.
>
> – Hebrews 10:35-39

Now more than ever, we are encouraged to not give up, to have confidence in the Lord. Now more than ever we need to persevere, feed on God's Word, and regain our strength, so that we can take Jesus' message of hope to the world.

CHEW ON THIS
What's causing you to shrink back spiritually? Are you

Shrink

stressed and anxious? Why or why not? What are you doing to prevent from losing your spiritual weight?

PRAYER
Lord, help me not to shrink back due to the stresses of this world. I want to be bold in my love for you and for others. Help me to fill myself daily with your Word, so that I can be strong and courageous and not give up.

DAY 23

Losing My Religion

GALATIANS 6:7
Do not be deceived: God cannot be mocked. A man reaps what he sows.

I have a confession to make. Although I love animals, I sometimes lose my religion when it comes to working with them. I may or may not have choked out a show goat (or two) that didn't want to walk (not to death . . . just a little choke). I may have also kicked a pig that wouldn't load in the trailer (word to the wise: hitting an animal with any part of your body tends to hurt your body more than the animal . . . just saying). I may have also thrown a rock at a horse that didn't want to be caught, and possibly a few other things that we don't speak of. I'm not

Losing My Religion

proud of any of these things; I'm just keeping it real. I will admit though, in the heat of the moment it felt . . . well . . . great! But just like all other sin, it only feels satisfying for a moment. Afterwards, well, that's a different story. First, regret sets in, and you feel like a scumbag because you've just tried to hurt a somewhat innocent animal. Second, I have three kids that have this sixth sense of knowing right when dad is losing it, and they tend to show up just in time to witness the whole offense. This leads to a whole other situation because, though I've quoted the famous line, "do as I say, not as I do," sadly, they tend to copy my behavior the next time an animal wants to act like an idiot. I don't know about you, but this is killer for me as a father. Especially because I want to set a godly example for my kids, but often times I fail.

Today's key verse is clear when it says that we will always reap what we sow. This scripture is not just true when it comes to our response to animals, it's true in every area of life. From how we spend our money, to the way we treat others, if we sow good seed, we will reap the rewards. For instance, if I choose to take a deep breath, practice some patience, and respond in a good way toward animals that aren't cooperating, then my kids tend to respond well, too, when it happens to them. On the bright side, my kids have made me a better father. Because their eyes are on me all the time, I'm learning

The Maker's Mark

to do what is right so that they can reap the benefits as well. I've also learned to humble myself and apologize to my kids when I've messed up . . . even when I've sinned against a pig.

What makes you lose your religion? Is it other people's driving? An incompetent waiter? Your pesky little brother? Cows? No matter what it is, we must remember that we can't control anyone else but ourselves, and if we want to reap God's blessing, then we must sow what is good and pleasing to Him.

CHEW ON THIS
In what area of your life are you sowing bad seed that could come back to bite you in the rear later? Who's watching how you respond to certain situations and what are your actions teaching them?

PRAYER
Lord, when I face the temptation to sow a bad seed, please help me to practice self-control and instead sow the right response. I want to do this in every area of my life and I want to set a godly example for everyone around me.

DAY 24

Are You Open?

1 JOHN 1:9
But if we confess our sins to him, he is faithful and just to forgive us our sins and to cleanse us from all wickedness. (NLT)

MATTHEW 7:16
You can identify them by their fruit, that is, by the way they act. Can you pick grapes from thornbushes, or figs from thistles? (NLT)

In the cattle business, open cows are not a good thing. You may be thinking, "What's an open cow?" Well, it's not a cow that is open-minded or easy to work with. It's actually a cow that's not pregnant. Why is this not good? It's not good because in the ranching industry, a cow's job is to produce a calf each year so that the ranch can sell that calf and hopefully make you some money. So, if the cow doesn't get pregnant and calve, you have no profit. You may also be thinking, "How do you know if a cow is open or not?" Well, each fall after the bulls have been pulled off the cows, the vet makes a visit to the ranch to preg check the cows. Most vets will palpate a cow to see if she is pregnant or open. I've also seen vets use an ultrasound/probing stick to see if a cow is open or pregnant. Preg checking cows is the most common way to tell if a cow is open or not, but it's not fool-proof. The more obvious sign that a cow is pregnant happens later, when eventually she begins to show. Her belly drops and when it's time to calve, she starts springing, and her udder swells up with milk. This shows that she's not open.

I would argue that the same is true when it comes to knowing Jesus. While we unfortunately have no way to spiritually "preg check" a person, I believe that a person that knows Christ personally should eventually start showing it. See, we all have this empty void in our lives that is never satisfied or filled until we give our lives to Jesus. Then, through the guidance of the Holy Spirit, we should begin to grow and show more compassion, more mercy, more patience, more peace, and more love. It should show in how we treat other people, how we interact with strangers, and how we love our enemies.

By now, you've read half of this devotional book, and hopefully it's caused you to think about your life and

Are You Open?

where you will spend eternity. Well, knowing your eternal destiny starts with knowing the answers to these simple questions: Am I open? Or is Christ living inside of me? If your answer is that you're open, then now is the time to ask Him to forgive you of your sin and be the Lord of your life. Today is your day to settle it once and for all! You say, "I don't really know how to give Him my life," well, today's key verse, 1 John 1:9, tells us how. It tells us to confess our sin to Jesus and ask for Him to forgive us. And when we do, He promises to set us free from our sin and make us new in Him. This is the most important decision we will ever make. So, if you're open, don't live another day without Christ in your life. Do it now!

To the person that claims to be a follower of Christ, I ask you this question: Does it show? In other words, is there any evidence that Jesus lives inside of you? There should be. The Bible says in Matthew 7:16 that we will know a person is a believer by the fruit they produce. Not only do we know that a cow is pregnant because it shows in her appearance, but we most definitely know she was pregnant when that baby is born. Her calf is the proof. For the believer, things like love, joy, peace, patience, kindness, goodness, and gentleness are the fruits that should come from us. Remember, we are not saved from our sin by what we do. We produce fruit and live for Him as a response to our salvation.

The Maker's Mark

CHEW ON THIS

Are you spiritually open? Do you know where you will spend eternity when you die? Do you need to accept Jesus' forgiveness and be saved today?

If you've already confessed to know Him, does it show in how you live your life? Commit today to let it show.

PRAYER

Prayer of Salvation: *Jesus, I know I'm a sinner. I know that no one else can save me but you. So, I'm asking for you to forgive my sin and come live in me. From this day forward, I will live for you. In Jesus' name I pray, Amen.*

Prayer of Commitment: *Lord, I know you're my Savior and Lord, but I really haven't shown that I love you to the world. I'm committing today to let it show in every area of my life. From the way I talk, to the way I make daily decisions, I'm going to live for you.*

DAY 25

Bucked Off Baron

LUKE 15:20
And while he was still a long way off, his father saw him coming. Filled with love and compassion, he ran to his son, embraced him, and kissed him. (NLT)

I got my first horse when I was in junior high. Because our family wasn't made of money and we really had no experience with horses, my dad had a friend find us a horse. He ended up finding us a half Quarter Horse, half Arabian bay gelding. Now while you may be thinking, "Good job on getting a gelding. But a half Quarter Horse, half Arabian? C'mon man." Looking back, I'd have to agree that he wasn't bred all that nice, but, at the time, I didn't care. He was my horse and I loved him. Being the humble kid that

The Maker's Mark

I was, I decided to name him after myself. That's right... I named him after myself (don't judge me, I was twelve). My middle name is Baron, so I thought, "I like my middle name, and so I'm going to name him Baron."

Well, wanting to be the best cowboy I could be, I asked the only other cowboy in my school for help. His name was Andy Bolton, and he and his dad roped a lot. I remember going to the Round-Up Club and helping turn out steers so they could practice their team roping. It was a blast. Andy and his dad, Larry, taught me everything I needed to know when it came to having a horse. They showed me how to brush him off, clean his hooves, and comb out his mane and tail. They helped me find a saddle and showed me how to saddle him correctly.

While all that was very helpful, what they failed to mention was that if I hadn't ridden him in a while, it would be best to warm him up before just getting on and loping off (you can see where this is headed). So, one day I decided I wanted to ride. I went out, caught Baron, and saddled him up. Not knowing any better, I just threw my leg over him and proceeded to trot across our pasture and up the pond dam. It wasn't until we were coming down the other side of the dam that I kicked Baron up into a lope. That's the last moment my butt was in the saddle. Baron split in two and yard darted me into the ground! I think I still have an indention in my cheek from

Bucked Off Baron

how hard I hit the ground! After the little white lights went away, I sat up and watched as my dad jumped the fence and came running across our pasture toward me. I'd never seen him run so fast. Being nearby, he heard the thud of me hitting the ground and wanted to make sure I was alright. He picked me up and dusted me off, and I remember feeling the love of my father that day.

This story reminds me of a story in the Bible where we see another father run to a son that had been "bucked off" a horse called life. The prodigal son, as he's called in Luke 15, thought the world had more to offer him than what he had at home. So, he asked his dad for his inheritance so he could leave home and live life his way. By asking for his inheritance early, he was essentially saying to his father, "I wish you were dead." But the father agreed to his son's request, and the boy ran off to a distant land where he lived "high on the hog." Soon after his money ran out, starving and looking for any way to feed himself, the son hired on with a pig farmer. There he found himself literally tempted to live like the hogs by eating their food. Coming to his senses, he decided to go back home to his father.

What the son couldn't have known, and what we can assume from what happens later in the story, is that every day the father waited and watched the road that led to his house, praying that his son would return. We can assume this because on the day that the son did return, the Bible tells us, "while he was still a long way off, his father saw him coming." And when he saw him, *he ran to his son* and kissed him.

These two stories are a perfect picture of God's love for you and me. Whether it's unintentional or intentional, we find ourselves knocked on our butts because of the poor choices we make. For example, maybe we make what we thought was a good financial investment, only to realize that it was a bad decision and we have to declare bankruptcy. Maybe we get around the wrong kind of friends and instead of us pulling them up to our standards, we get dragged down to theirs. We get tempted to chase the money and success at work, and we find our family falling apart at the seams. What we must never forget is that no matter how we get bucked off, God is always running toward us, ready to heal our hurt and welcome us back home.

CHEW ON THIS

What bad choices have you made that you think that God won't forgive? What's keeping you from coming back to Jesus and having a right relationship with Him again? Turn to Him today. Accept His forgiveness. And enjoy the joy of being in a right relationship with Him again.

Bucked Off Baron

PRAYER

Dear God, forgive me for the ways I've chosen not to honor you. Heal my past. And when I fail again, help me to trust your love for me. Thank you for loving me so much.

DAY 26

Farm Weld

COLOSSIANS 1:17
He is before all things, and in him all things hold together.

Living the ranching lifestyle isn't always about getting to saddle a good horse each day and ride through cattle. Some of the best hands I've been around knew more than just how to sit a horse. In my opinion, one skill that makes a person pretty handy is knowing how to weld. Now, I'm the first to admit that I'm not a good welder. I don't know things like why a 7018 welding rod is better than 6010 or 6011; I've just been told that it's better. I don't know what type rod is made for welding up or which rod is made for welding down. But I have mastered the art of what most guys commonly refer to as a "farm weld." This is a weld that isn't at all pretty, but it holds whatever it is you're welding together so you can use it

Farm Weld

to get a job done.

Not too long ago, some friends of mine and I were welding up some continuous fence for another guy. One of the guys, who happens to be a great welder, watched as I did my best to lay down a pretty weld. Seeing that I didn't really know what I was doing, he kindly offered some pointers. He told me things like, "when you're welding top-rail to your line posts, you need to tilt your rod up a bit," and "when welding a vertical seam, you need to speed up a little and come back and weld over what you just welded." But it wasn't until he said, "loosen your grip and relax your arm," that I began to weld the best I'd ever welded. See, I was so tense, partly because I knew he was watching me but also because I felt like I had to have a tight grip on the handle to control the rod and make a good weld. What I quickly learned was that the opposite was true. The looser my grip and the more relaxed my arm was, the smoother my hand moved, making my welds prettier and stronger.

Sometimes I treat my life a lot like my welding. I think that as long as I have a tight grip on the things that are happening around me, life is going to be good. Sadly, this couldn't be further from the truth. What I learn more and more every day is that just like welding with a loose grip makes for a smoother weld, life is always better, and in many cases a lot smoother, when I loosen my grip and allow God to guide my every move. This is a real struggle for me because I want to control everything. For example, I want to keep a tight grip on my kids. I want to keep a tight grip on the people that work for me. I want to control how people respond to my preaching. I want to control how I spend my time. I want to control how my wife responds to my hints for getting frisky (can I get a witness). I want to control everything. But as I've already admitted, the more I try to control things and not let God have control, the less I grow, and the more things go south.

Maybe you're like me and you want to have a tight grip on everything. Maybe you have a tight grip on a dating relationship that you don't want to end. Or maybe you have a tight grip on where you want to work or live. Maybe you have a tight grip on your money. We all struggle with holding on to things too tightly. But if we were wise and knew what was best for us, we would listen to our Lord's instruction in today's key verse and trust that He holds all things together. Looking back on that day of welding, I would've never made a better weld if I hadn't listened to my friend. He was more experienced. He was encouraging. He made me better. God is the same way. He doesn't want to control us because He's this controlling God who doesn't want us to live a great life. He wants control so that we can succeed and live a more fulfilling life—a life of peace, joy, and purpose.

Farm Weld

CHEW ON THIS
What do you need to loosen your grip on and allow God to guide you in? What are you trying to make happen that's not working? How teachable are you? Are you willing to surrender everything to the Lord?

PRAYER
God, I don't want to control my life, so I'm surrendering everything to you. Thank you for being an all-knowing, all-powerful God that knows what's best for me. I trust you and I commit to doing things your way.

DAY 27

Relentless

MATTHEW 5:6
Blessed are those who hunger and thirst for righteousness, for they will be filled.

LUKE 16:10
If you are faithful in little things, you will be faithful in large ones. (NLT)

While I don't know Trevor Brazile personally, it's hard not to respect a man who's won twenty-four world titles in the sport of rodeo. He's won the world in the steer roping, tie-down roping, and team roping, but the majority of his world titles came by winning fourteen All-Around Cowboy World Championships. While all of this quite impressive and unmatched in the sport, the thing I admire most about Trevor's accomplishments is that he won most of them back-to-back. This means that after winning a title

Relentless

once, he won it again the next year. Trevor won his first back-to-back All-Around titles from 2002–2004. He then went on a streak of winning ten All-Around world titles back-to-back from 2006–2015. Why is this so impressive to me? For many reasons, but what impresses me the most is Trevor's ability to stay hungry and at the top of his sport, even after so many wins. I've heard it said, and I believe it to be true, that the greatest threat to future success is current success. In other words, more often than not, success leads to complacency, and complacency leads to failure.

While I don't know exactly what all went into Trevor winning so many titles, the name of his clothing and tack brand, Relentless, gives me a pretty good indication. I would imagine that these titles didn't happen because Trevor made one or two big decisions that made all the difference, but that he was relentless in making small day-to-day decisions, leading him to accomplish such amazing results. For Trevor to stay hungry and winning, it probably meant waking up early, saddling horses, and putting in the practice every day. It probably meant instead of staying up late, he chose to go to bed early. It meant working on his horsemanship, and feeding and caring for his horses every day. I'm sure it meant choosing to embrace the grind of the road. Traveling mile after mile, to rodeo after rodeo, making run after run, all to earn the money it took to qualify for the NFR year after year. These decisions and more are what I believe has led to Trevor's success in rodeo.

The closest I can come to relating to what Trevor has done year after year is that I've had the privilege of serving the Lord in ministry back-to-back for over two decades. And, like Trevor, I'd say the credit goes to the relentless commitment to making thousands of small choices day after day that has helped me win year after year in ministry. What do I mean by winning? That's simple—winning is seeing people's lives changed by Jesus week after week, month after month, and year after year. Winning is making it to my wedding day a virgin. Winning is not being addicted to porn, alcohol, or drugs. Winning is remaining faithful to my wife for going on fifteen years. Winning is raising kids that love Jesus and love His church. Winning is not quitting or giving up when things got hard. I believe that these things continue to happen as a result of the hundreds of smaller, consistent, behind-the-scenes decisions I've chosen to make every day. What kind of decisions? Praying daily and reading God's Word morning and evening. The decision to get out of bed, eat healthy, get good rest, and study hard. The decision to pursue Christ-centered friendships. The decision to not just hang with church people, but to be a friend of sinners. These decisions have all led to me serving the Lord faithfully back-to-back-to-back. Don't get me wrong, I've made lots of wrong decisions too, but what I've learned from the lives of so many other faithful followers of Christ is: winning comes from the things you do consistently that no one else sees—that leads to the results that everyone wants.

What about you? Are you making decisions daily that are helping you win in business, at home, and in your spiritual life? As our key verse tells us, God wants us to hunger and thirst for righteousness. When we stay hungry and put in the work, He promises that we will be blessed.

CHEW ON THIS
What decisions are you making today that are leading you to be successful tomorrow? What area of your spiritual life do you need to be more consistent in? What can you look back on in your life that has contributed to your greatest success?

PRAYER
Lord, I want to be relentless in my pursuit of you. I want to do what it takes to win the battles I face every day, and succeed at pleasing you. Help me to make decisions every day that honor you and lead me to fulfill my purpose.

DAY 28

We Call Him Fingers

LUKE 18:14
For all those who exalt themselves will be humbled, and those who humble themselves will be exalted.

We've all been around him. You know who I'm talking about . . . he's the guy with the new knife in his pocket that's never had blood on it. The guy who bought used leggings to make it look like he's done some work. The guy with tie strings on his swells, hobbles hanging from his D-ring, and taps on his stirrups. Looking at him, you might think he's a hand, but, while all of this may make him look like a hand, we call him *Fingers*, 'cause he ain't no hand.

To be honest, I don't have a problem with this guy.

We Call Him Fingers

Why? Because, at one point, I was that guy (some of my friends would say I'm still that guy . . . but they can shut it). Just because you don't have a lot of experience cowboyin' or riding a horse doesn't make you a bad guy, it just means you're green, which is really no big deal. What I do have a problem with is when Fingers *talks* like he knows what he's doing. "Oh yeah, I can rope. I've been cowboying for a while. I grew up on a ranch back home." But then you ask him to do a job, and he's a wreck waiting to happen. I probably shouldn't say this, but I kind of enjoy watching posers like Fingers get their butts handed to them because, in some ways, they ask for it by running their mouth (that's probably not very Christian, but it's true). What's even more tragic is that a guy like Fingers not only can hurt himself, but he can put others in a bad spot, too, because of his dishonesty.

If I've learned one thing about cowboys, it's that they tend to respect a guy who can admit he doesn't know how to do something and actually asks for help. This act of humility makes a good hand more willing to help a guy like Fingers.

I remember the first time my friend Marshall asked me to drag calves at his branding. I reluctantly answered, "Heck no, you don't want me to drag. You'll be waiting a while 'cause I don't know what I'm doing." But he didn't care. He said, "It's ok, just give it a try. We'll help you." So,

The Maker's Mark

I did, and, while I didn't rope great that day, I've got the pictures to prove that I did catch a few. Marshall and I have talked about this since, and he 100 percent agrees, "We will help anyone who is willing to learn. But if a dude shows up running his mouth, we might lead him out a bronc and tell him it's gentle, just to humble him a little."

When it comes to serving God, we are told to have this same teachable attitude. He doesn't care if you've never done something, He just wants you to be humble and willing to try. Maybe you've never prayed out loud. It's ok to admit to God that you're scared. He understands and He wants to help you get past that fear. Maybe you've never told someone about Jesus and how He can change their life. You think they might make fun of you or you won't have the right words to say in the moment. It's ok! Give your fear to God. Ask Him to give you the words at just the right moment and then give it a try. No matter how long you've been a follower of Christ, there is always something you can learn. I've been around a lot of self-righteous Christians who are a lot like Fingers. They think they have it all figured out and they hide their doubts and fears to try and make themselves look more spiritual.

What I've learned about people is that those who are far from Christ can never relate to perfection. In other words, when we act like we don't have any problems or face any doubts about God, we distance ourselves from those who do have problems or a past that they're not proud of. What I've come to realize is that it's our weakness that connects us to our neighbors, not our strength. Therefore, we would all do ourselves a favor if we'd just be honest about our weaknesses and be willing to admit we don't have it all together. This is what God blesses, and, just like a good hand is willing to help a guy who's humble, God is more willing and able to use a person who walks in humility.

CHEW ON THIS

When was the last time you were honest with God? When was the last time you were honest with those around you and asked for help? What's an area of your life that you need to be honest and admit you're weak in and ask someone to help you get stronger?

PRAYER

Jesus, I know I don't have it all together, so I'm asking you to help me grow in my faith, my love, my obedience, and my humility. I don't want to bring any undue pain on myself or anyone else because I'm not being honest. Thank you for your willingness to use me in spite of my weakness.

DAY 29

The Underdog

LUKE 18:27
Jesus replied, "What is impossible with man is possible with God."

EPHESIANS 3:20
Now all glory to God, who is able, through his mighty power at work within us, to accomplish infinitely more than we might ask or think. (NLT)

I've always loved being the underdog. Whether in a wrestling match, in preaching, or when it comes to cowboying, I love it when I surprise someone by what I can get done. Now, I'm the first to admit that I'm not the best at any of these things but, when it comes to roping and dragging calves, I have been known to have a good day every now and then. I often get invited to a ranch to take pictures of

The Underdog

families and cowboys at work. Often times, there are new cowboys that come to help and they don't know me from Adam. So, they naturally suspect that I'm just there to get some good pics for the mothers and wives to enjoy. But then I get asked to help drag and, much to their surprise (and mine sometimes), I'm actually able to make a hand.

I remember being invited to the Reed Ranch in Spearman, Texas. I usually spend most of my time taking pics of the great cowboys that work for the Reeds, but on occasion they let me drag a few calves. On one particular occasion, I actually roped pretty well and I remember A.D. Reed, the ranch's patriarch and top hand, came up to me afterwards to tell me that I had the guys talking about how impressed they were with my dragging skills. While it was nice to hear that and humbling at the same time, to me the biggest reward came from being able to out-perform their expectations. While I'd like to take credit for being able to get done what I did, I can tell you the secret to always out-performing others' expectations. The secret is having God on your side.

Here's what I've learned from riding with Christ: In the eyes of others, you may seem like an underdog, but with Christ you can do the impossible. It may seem that you're not smart enough to go to college, but with Christ you can do it. It may seem that you're not good enough to get that job. But with Christ you can not only get the job, but after a while you can get the promotion, and then eventually become the boss. You may think, "that hot babe over there would never fall in love with a guy like me." Take it from me, God can blind her enough to look past your ugly mug and see what a great guy you are, and y'all could end up living happily ever after.

See, what a lot of people don't get is: without Jesus, we are nothing and we can accomplish nothing of true worth. But with Christ, we can do anything He asks us to do. You could be a high-school dropout. It doesn't matter. With Christ in your corner, you can do the impossible. As a parent you may think to yourself, "I have no idea how to be a good dad." Well, let me tell you, even though my grandpa died when my dad was four years old, my dad had another Heavenly Father to help him become the greatest dad I've ever known. God can equip you to be an outstanding parent, and, where you're lacking, God can fill the gaps.

If you think about it, Jesus was underdog too. Sure, He was the Son of God, but not everyone believed that. Even His own brother didn't believe He was special. He just looked at Him as his kid-brother and not the Savior of the world that He was. To many of His own followers, Jesus wasn't what they thought He'd be. Instead of conquering the Romans and becoming the King of Israel like everyone hoped He would, Jesus sought no throne, had

The Underdog

no crown or palace, but instead a pair of sandals and a mission to do His Father's will. And against all odds, that's exactly what He did. He out-performed everyone around Him by loving the unlovable, healing the sick, performing miracle after miracle, and eventually even defeating death. This Underdog changed the world!

So, if He can do all these things and more, surely He can help you do more than you could have ever dreamed or thought you could do. If the odds are against you, take hope. God is in the business of using underdogs. And God wants to use an underdog just like you.

CHEW ON THIS
What's holding you back from being who God wants you to be? Is it your past? Your fears? What mindset or habit do you need to get rid of to begin to be used by God in ways you never thought possible?

PRAYER
Jesus, I thank you for empowering me to do the impossible. I trust that you want to use me and I'm giving you permission. Take what little I have and use it to out-perform what anyone thought was possible. I give you the glory and honor.

DAY 30

Walking on a Loose Rein

MARK 5:27,29
She had heard about Jesus, so she came up behind him through the crowd and touched his robe . . . Immediately the bleeding stopped, and she could feel in her body that she had been healed of her terrible condition. (NLT)

Just before my wife's grandfather passed away, he gave her a little filly that we call Tucker. Because she was a gift from such a special man, Tucker's pretty special to us. On top of that, she's the first horse I ever started. Although she's a mare, and I'm not too high on mares, I like her because she's tough, gentle, and has a big heart. But there is one thing that she has never been good at, and that's walking on a loose rein. I've tried everything to break

Walking on a Loose Rein

her of this habit, from running her wide open for miles in deep sand to dragging logs. I've tried pulling her head around to my knee thousands of times, trying to teach her: when you trot, you get to feel pressure, but when you walk, you don't. She's pushing sixteen years old now, and nothing has worked. You might be thinking, "Trotting is a good thing when you have a job to get done, right?" Well, this may be true when you have a lot of ground to cover, but when you just want to slowly gather or push cattle, it's the worst. It's also terrible when you're just out for a ride with your kids or your bae, and she wants to trot away from everyone.

For me, the benefits of a horse that can walk on a loose rein are many. First off, it just looks nice. Watching a horse put its head down and walk out is a fine sight to see. I've also found that walking and not trotting in many cases is safer. I've been in tall grass that hides deep ditches made by runoff water, and if you're not watching and your horse is trotting out at a pretty good pace, you can both get in a bind pretty quickly. Another benefit is: when your horse is just walking, you're less likely to miss cattle or calves when you're gathering them. Not to mention, when your horse is willing to just walk, you can visit easier with your buddies.

I believe that Jesus wants us to be like a horse that walks on a loose rein. Why? Because Jesus Himself knew

The Maker's Mark

the value and benefits that came from not being in a hurry. Think about it . . . He would have never seen or been able to minister to the people He was called to serve if He was always in a hurry. He wouldn't have had time to feed the 5,000 or eat with sinners. He wouldn't have had time to teach His disciples or heal the sick. Our key verse comes from a story in the Bible about a woman who had suffered from constant bleeding for twelve years. She had tried everything to get better, but nothing worked. Until one day, she heard about how Jesus had been healing others and that He was actually coming through her town. Having faith that He could heal her, she came up behind Him through the crowd and touched Jesus' robe. Instantly, she was healed from her bleeding.

Now, I know the point of this story is that the woman's faith helped her find healing, but I want to point out something that you may have never noticed before. The reason the woman was able to be healed that day was because Jesus was *walking*, not running. How do we know that He was walking? Because if you read the verse, it mentions that the woman came up behind Him through the crowd. I don't know about you, but the times I've been in a big crowd, with people touching me from every direction, it's been nearly impossible to run. Therefore, I would argue that Jesus was walking and not running. Another indication that Jesus was walking was that He felt her touch. It says later in the same chapter that Jesus realized that healing power had gone out from Him and He turned around and asked, "Who touched my robe?" (Mark 5:30, NLT). His disciples were like . . . *Can you not see this crowd pressing around you? How can you ask for one specific person that touched you when there are so many?* Again, I'd argue that because Jesus was walking and not in a hurry, He felt the woman's touch.

What's the point? I'll speak for myself and admit that I often find myself in a hurry and not able to see and serve those around me. It's sad but true. And even more sobering is that this is where the devil loves for us to be. Sure, he tries to stop us from doing God's will, but what I've learned is that if he can't stop you, he will get behind you and push you so fast that you don't have time to do God's will. So, what's the answer? In a world that constantly says to hustle, hurry, strive, I believe God has called us to walk on a loose rein, allowing Him to control how fast or slow we move toward fulfilling His will.

CHEW ON THIS

In what area(s) of your life has the devil gotten behind you and pushed you so fast you weren't able to do God's will? What can you start doing today that will allow you to slow down and serve others better? What do you need

The Maker's Mark

to let go of to give you more time to serve God?

PRAYER

Jesus, I want to be available and ready at any time to obey you. Help me to figure out the stride you want me in, so that I can see what you see and do what you want me to do.

DAY 31

Listen to Your Ass

NUMBERS 22:28
And the LORD opened the mouth of the ass ... (KJV)

One of the funniest comedians on the planet is a guy named Bill Engvall. Being a Texas boy, he knows what it's like to live the country life and pokes fun at all the things country folk do. For years he did this bit called "Here's Your Sign." In it, he makes fun of some of the stupid questions or statements we make and how, when we make these statements, we deserve a sign that warns others of our ignorance. I'd write some of them here, but it wouldn't be that funny. I encourage you to google it, but be warned: if you don't have a sense of humor or you're pretty sensitive to others poking fun at your flubs, you'll

The Maker's Mark

probably be offended. Take it from a guy who says some pretty stupid stuff sometimes and deserves a sign every now and then . . . it's ok to laugh at yourself!

I think all of us in our day-to-day lives face situations, questions, or decisions and because we want to make the right decision, we ask God for a sign. We ask Him to speak to us or at least give us some sort of sign to confirm that what we're doing is either right or wrong. Well, I for one believe that God desires to speak to us. Sure, He is quiet sometimes to help build our faith, but the majority of the time He gives us the answers we need to make wise decisions. The questions that come up are: what do we have to do to hear from Him? And how does He speak? I'll answer the first question by making some pretty obvious statements: First, for us to hear from God, *we must know Jesus personally.* The Bible says in John 8:47, "Whoever belongs to God hears what God says . . ." This means if we want to hear from God, we have to belong to Him. How do we belong to Him? We give Him our life by trusting in His Son, Jesus. Secondly, to hear from God *we must listen.* Seriously though, if we are doing all the talking and not listening, then we will not hear what God has to say to us. I've spent a lot of time around people that are unchurched and I've noticed that when I say things like, "God told me I needed to do this" or "God spoke to me and said this is what I want you to do . . ." They get this

Listen to Your Ass

weird look on their face like, "How does God say those things?" or "How does He speak?" Well, I'd say He speaks to us however He wants to speak. God has no limits on what He can do or how He wants to do it; therefore, He can speak in whatever way He desires.

For example, there's a story in the Bible in the book of Numbers, chapter twenty-two, about a prophet named Balaam. A king named Balak needed a prophet to help him defeat his enemy, so he sent his messengers to offer the prophet Balaam a bunch of money to put a curse on his opponents. Balaam says no the first time, but then the messengers come back and God tells Balaam to go with them. Somehow, through Balaam's greediness, God gets ticked at him and tries to stop him along the way by sending an angel with his sword to kill Balaam. Problem is, Balaam can't see the angel, but his donkey can. So, his donkey first ducks off the path; then she threw herself and Balaam into a wall, crushing Balaam's foot; and lastly the donkey just laid down on Balaam. It was after Balaam smote (beat) his ass (literally . . . beat his . . . well you get the point), that the Bible says in verse 28, "And the LORD opened the mouth of the ass, and she said to Balaam . . ." Did you just hear what that verse said? The Lord spoke through a jackass. You can't make this stuff up . . . it's right there in the Bible. The point is, if God can speak through a jackass, He can speak through anything. I could go on

The Maker's Mark

and on about how He spoke through different signs to other people in the Bible, like when He spoke through a burning bush to Moses, a cloud to the Israelites, an angel to Mary, and a fleece to Gideon. So, just remember: don't limit God or be afraid to ask God for a sign, but always keep your eyes on Him, and once He speaks, obey.

CHEW ON THIS
Are you able to hear the voice of God? Do you belong to Him? When was the last time God spoke to you? How did He speak to you? What sign is God asking you to ask for so that He can direct your decisions?

PRAYER
Lord, I know I have your Word to direct my path. And I thank you for the Holy Spirit who lives inside of me to guide me. Thank you for your willingness to show me a sign and speak to me when I need the answers to questions in life. Help me to not only hear your voice, but to obey it.

DAY 32

Grit Don't Quit

2 CHRONICLES 15:7
But as for you, be strong and do not give up, for your work will be rewarded. (NLT)

If you've ever had the privilege of dragging calves with a great group of guys/gals, you know that for most cowboys, this job is their dream job. I've been fortunate enough to drag hundreds of calves to the fire, and I can tell you that, from my perspective, there's nothing more exciting. If you've not had the pleasure of working calves this way, then you may not even know what I'm talking about. So, let me explain. Dragging calves refers to when you have a set of calves in a pen, and a cowboy that's horseback rides into the group of calves, throws a loop around the calf's back legs, pulls his slack, dallies the rope around his saddle horn, and drags the calf to the crew to be worked. This is a time-honored tradition that,

The Maker's Mark

as I stated earlier, most cowboys live for. Well, as you can imagine, when it comes to working with cattle, things don't always go the way you want them to go.

For instance, while day-working with some friends of mine, I was asked to be a part of the ground crew. So, as a cowboy would bring a calf to us, our job was to get the calf on its side so that it could be worked with as little stress as possible. Then we would let it up so that it could return to the herd. Well, my job on this day was to grab the calf's tail and pull it toward the ground (i.e. tail the calf), while the other guy's job was to grab the rope and lift, thereby causing the calf to be flanked on its side. Done right, this would allow us to get ahold of it so it could be tagged, vaccinated, branded, cut if necessary, and wormed. With a great crew, this works smoothly and everyone is able to do their job with ease.

Well, this one particular time, one of the guys roped a big soggy calf and proceeded to bring him to my partner and me. Unfortunately, when the calf got to us, we didn't get him flanked the first try, which allowed the calf to kick one foot out of the rope and commence to wrap himself and the rope around me. (In our defense, the calf probably weighed a good 350 pounds, my partner weighed maybe 135 pounds soaking wet, and my grip on the tail may not have been as good as it should have been.) Well, not being a quitter and not wanting to get made fun of by

Grit Don't Quit

the other guys for getting whipped by this calf, I clamped onto this calf's front leg like a vice grip. What I didn't realize, was that the rest of the crew was trying to flank the calf but couldn't because I had ahold of the calf's leg. It wasn't until one of the guys said, "Let go!" that I finally opened my grip and let the guys flank him. I immediately jumped up and said, "What took y'all so long! I was just waiting for someone to call me off." Although I earned the nickname "Lock Jaw," I felt good that day because, even though I lost the battle the first time, I didn't quit until the job got done.

Similar to not quitting that calf, one of the things I've observed in life is that, as humans, we are never truly defeated when we lose a battle. We're defeated when we quit. For example, we lose a battle and look at something on the internet that we shouldn't have. Sure, we may have lost the battle that day, but it doesn't mean we should just quit trying and give in to it again and again. That's dumb. It's always better to confess it to the Lord, allow Him to forgive you, and fight the next battle and win. For you, it may be that you're trying to eat healthy. But one day you give into temptation and eat that king-size Reese's and drink that 32oz Slurpee from 7-Eleven. So what! Make the next meal a healthy one and keep moving forward in your desire to get healthy. The point is, just because you lose one battle doesn't mean you're done. Get back up and recommit to fight another day.

Let me say this as well. Sometimes to others, letting go of something like a dream, a relationship, or a job may look like quitting when it's simply an act of obedience. Just like my buddy called me off that calf and told me to let go so they could finish the job, God sometimes calls us to stop certain things so that He can finish the job. Don't ever be afraid to obey, even if it looks to others like you're quitting. God knows what He's doing, so trust Him.

CHEW ON THIS

What are you thinking about quitting that you know God has told you to stick out and not give up on? What area of your life have you lost a battle, and you need to recommit to Christ and get back to honoring Him in? Maybe God is calling you out of a situation so that He can do something even greater through you. Are you willing to trust Him no matter what others may think?

PRAYER

Lord, I don't want to quit anything you want me to be a part of. If this means I need to stay hooked where you have me planted, I'm willing. But Lord, if you are calling me off of something because you have some other plan for me, I want to be obedient to do that as well. Show me your will

Grit Don't Quit

and give me the strength to follow you wherever you lead.

DAY 33

The Good Old Days

ECCLESIASTES 7:10
Don't long for "the good old days." This is not wise. (NLT)

I talk to people all the time that mention how they long for the good old days. And with certain things, I'm right there with them. Things like: I want to always use horses to gather cattle and not four wheelers. I want to buy handmade gear versus factory made. I think a wood fire is better than a gas fire, and I admire a good team of horses and a chuckwagon. But what I've learned about change is that the one thing you can count on in life is that things are going to change.

I see so many people who refuse to change, and it saddens me. They say things like, "The internet is from the

The Good Old Days

devil. These blasted cell phones are ruining our kids. I hate texting, I'd just rather someone call me. Instagram, Twitter, and Facebook are all a waste of time." Or maybe it's something at church that changes, "Why's that pastor preaching from a screen rather than in person? We don't need projector screens and computers. That's for those fancy mega-churches." Tragically, what I've seen firsthand in the church is that *what we avoid, the devil invades.* In other words, if the church just sticks their heads up their butts and doesn't take advantage of these things, the devil will.

I look at social media and cell phones, and sure you can find a lot of evil things on them. But what about the way we can reach the world with the good news of Jesus Christ with just click of a button. I've often thought that if the Apostle Paul, the writer of most of the New Testament, was to return to earth and find me not taking advantage of the technology I have at my finger-tips, he'd punch me in the face and say, "You idiot! I had to ride a donkey to get the word out about Jesus. All you have to do is click a button and you won't do it? You fool!" You may say, "Paul wouldn't say those harsh things." Have you read the Bible? He'd say those things and maybe use a few other expletives to describe our ignorance.

I can't tell you how many life-giving conversations I've had with cowboys via texting. We've talked about their struggling marriage, their depression, the Bible, and their eternity. What I've learned is that texting is so much less threatening to a lot of guys, and they often times can say things in a text that they'd never share in person. For me, I'll take seeing people's lives changed however I can get it.

By the way, God embraced change too. After He used the flood to purge the earth of sin and the ark to save Noah, He shelved it and said, "I'm not going to use that method again." He used lambs as sacrifices for our sins in the Old Testament, but then He said, "I'm done with that, I'm going to sacrifice my own Son once and for all." He dwelt in temples for a while. Then a cloud. Then fire. But then He shelved those methods, and now He lives in the heart of every believer.

As Christ-centered leaders of our families, leaders in the church, and leaders in our community, we would do well to change *how* we reach the world. We would be smart to not only ask, "What would those who've gone before me do?" but to also ask the question, "What would my successor do?" This will not only assure that we reach the next generation and keep the church relevant to the world God has called us to reach, but it will also please God. By us setting aside our pride and ego and replacing them with a willingness to learn new ways to grow the kingdom of God, we will not get left in the dust and allow the devil to

The Good Old Days

take more ground.

CHEW ON THIS

What attitude or view of something do you need to change in your life so that God can use you more effectively to reach the lost? What idea or method do you need to embrace and learn to love so that the next generation isn't ruled by the devil? What are you avoiding that the devil has invaded?

PRAYER

Dear God, I want to be who you want me to be and I want to reach the world you have me in. Help me to make the necessary changes in my attitude towards change and take action in reaching the culture around me that so desperately needs you.

DAY 34

Shift Happens

PHILIPPIANS 1:12
And I want you to know, my dear brothers and sisters, that everything that has happened to me here has helped to spread the Good News. (NLT)

For years, I have loved starting my own colts. One part of a colt's training is teaching them to yield to pressure and become soft and supple. For instance, when training a colt, I might bend his head around and hold it as many times as it takes for as long as it takes until he decides to give to the pressure and soften. Every horse is different, but after practicing this method for a few sessions, most colts experience a shift in their brain. They eventually decide to go from pulling on you and resisting the pressure, to understanding that when they are soft and give into the pressure, they find release and life is better.

Shift Happens

One of the things I've learned in life is that, much like a colt learning to think differently about what is happening to him so he can become a great horse, I have to learn to think differently about the pressures that God allows in my life so that I can become who He wants me to be.

Paul, the writer of today's key verse, knew the power of shifting his focus off of his circumstances and onto what God was doing in and through him. For example, in the book of Philippians, which ironically most Bible scholars would say is a book about joy, we find Paul writing his letter to the church in Philippi while sitting in prison chained to a guard. I don't know about you, but that doesn't sound like a very joy-filled place to be. But what Paul was learning to do was to allow God to change the way he viewed his circumstances. These things weren't happening to him for no reason. They were happening so that he could find true joy no matter what pressure he faced, and so the gospel could spread.

So many of us tend to focus on the pain, the discomfort, and the struggle, instead of focusing on who God is and how He is using our current situation to spread his goodness. See, Paul could have considered himself a hostage in prison, but he didn't. He viewed his circumstance as an opportunity to spread the gospel to those he was chained to, those in the prison cell next door, and those who he was writing to.

The Maker's Mark

CHEW ON THIS

What pressure are you facing today? Do you need to shift your view of your current circumstance? Do you need to give into the fact that God is in control and that He is using you to make a difference for Him?

PRAYER

Lord, please shift my focus from what's happening all around me to what's happening in and through me. Help me to know that no matter what pressures I face in life, you are always working in them to spread your love and forgiveness.

DAY 35

Stripping Perfection

PHILIPPIANS 3:12
I don't mean to say that I have already achieved these things or that I have already reached perfection. But I press on to possess that perfection for which Christ Jesus first possessed me. (NLT)

One of my favorite places to day-work is the Smith/Oasis Ranch in Canadian, Texas. My good friend Marshall Long is the ranch manager there and we've had lots of great experiences working together. I had the pleasure of seeing Marshall come to know Christ and I got to baptize him in a river just north of where we lived. I've never told him this, but, while I may have played a small part in mentoring him spiritually, he's been my greatest influence when it comes to cowboyin'. He's the greatest hand I've ever ridden with, and, for the most part, he expects his crew to be great hands as well. That said, to be asked to come and work for him is a true honor.

A few years back, I was helping Marshall with his spring works. We had gathered a couple sets of cows and worked the first set when Marshall hollered at me and a few other guys to take the second set of cows and strip the mommas off the calves. This meant that we needed to sort the momma cows from their calves so that we could run the mommas through the chute and drag the calves. Although this job is commonly done in the gate afoot, this particular day we decided to do it horseback. This meant that while the other cowboys were bringing the cows and calves to the gate to be sorted, one of us had to stand in the gate horseback, letting the cows go by but not the calves. Sounds difficult, right? Well, it is. I remember one of the cowboys looked at the other guy and said, "There's no way I can sort them on my horse, he's only got about ninety days on him, and it wouldn't be pretty." Then the other cowboy piped up and said, "My horse won't do any good either." Then they both looked at me, and one of them said, "You're up, Beau!"

Now if you've ever had to sort cows this way, you know that it says something about a cowboy when he can sort cattle horseback. Needless to say, you kind of

Stripping Perfection

have to know what you're doing, and more importantly you have to have a horse that's broke. If I was being honest, although I knew my horse was handy enough to do the job, in that moment, I felt I was not. But, because I've always had a hunger to get better at what I do, I stepped into the gate and told the boys to bring 'em to me. I wish I could tell you that I was perfect that day and not a single calf got by me, but that wouldn't be true. The truth is, although I was successful at keeping eighty or so calves from getting through, I did let a couple get by. And although the guys told me I did a good job, boy did I hate not being perfect.

Later that day, Marshall and I were watering down the corrals for the next day's branding. While we were visiting, I told him that when he asked me to strip those cows, I wanted so badly to do it perfectly. I told him that I hated letting him down and really didn't know why he trusted me to do such a crucial job. Much to my surprise and relief, he looked at me and said, "It's ok—letting a few calves by is more fun anyway, because the guys get to go rope them and drag them back out." I was like, "*Thank you, Jesus!*" Here I was worried about disappointing my boss and friend, when he didn't really expect me to be perfect in the first place. All he asked was for me to get in there and try.

I bet you if I were to ask him now about that day, he'd

probably tell me that he knew I wasn't going to be perfect before I even stepped into the gate. He'd known this because he knows that some days everything goes right, and some days it doesn't. The fact is, he chose me to work for him *before* I failed and he chose me to work for him *after* I failed. Why? Because he likes me, not because I am perfect, but because I tried, I put in effort.

Spiritually speaking, although God knows we will never be perfect, He still asks us to strive for perfection anyway. Why? Because it's in *trying* that we change the world. He's not so concerned about us falling short, He just asks each of us to do our best. Some days that means we do things well, and some days that means we don't. The truth is, God has called all of us to do a job. It may be a job that we feel we're inadequate to do or a job we fear we're going to fail at. But just like my buddy Marshall used me in spite of my failures, God wants to use us in spite of our failures also. Today's key verse tells us we are called to strive for perfection, but, let's be real, none of us will ever be perfect. But hear me when I say, that's no excuse to not strive for it!

The next day we got up and gathered another set of cows, got them in the pens, and Marshall stepped into the gate on his great horse Paint. Out of 119 pairs, Marshall and Paint stripped every cow perfectly—not letting one calf get by. It was so much fun to watch them accomplish

Stripping Perfection

perfection that I lost sight of my own imperfection. In that moment, I was just happy to be in the same pen as them.

This is true with Jesus too. His perfection covers our imperfection. And get this: Jesus Christ wasn't just perfect one day—He was perfect his whole life! God sent His only Son, Jesus, to earth to live a perfect life, only to die a miserable death. Why? So that our imperfections, our sin, and our failures could be covered. Remember this: Even though we serve a perfect God, He uses imperfect people to fulfill His perfect will. Praise Jesus!

CHEW ON THIS

Are you allowing your fear of failure to keep you from doing your best for God? Are you allowing your past to hold you back? Today's the day to start striving again. Not for acceptance or to work your way into heaven, but in response to what all Jesus has done for you. Get your eyes off of your imperfection and place them on the only perfect person to ever walk the face of the earth, Jesus.

PRAYER

Jesus, thank you for being my perfect Savior. Thank you for challenging me to strive to be the best that I can be. I give you my sin, my failure, and my fear, and I ask that you would help me to press on and fulfill the purpose you have

The Maker's Mark

for me. I'm ready to give you my best.

DAY 36

Forgiving My Cowgirl

1 CORINTHIANS 13:7
Love never gives up, never loses faith, is always hopeful, and endures through every circumstance. (NLT)

We've raised our three kids around horses and cattle in hopes that they'd fall in love with the ranching way of life and want to carry on the tradition. There's just something about getting your hands dirty and sweating a little that makes life better, and we want our kids to love it too. But when my daughter, Madeline, was around seven or eight years old, I thought these dreams were shattered. I had invited her to go for a ride with me, and, much to my disappointment and shock, she looked back at me and said, "Dad, I don't like riding horses and I never want to

The Maker's Mark

ride them again." Ouch. It was like she stabbed me in the back and then twisted the knife a little. I was heartbroken to say the least. Here we had invested in some of the best kid horses in the country, bought saddles to fit each kid, and had started building our own herd for her to one day build upon, but she dropped a bomb on those dreams. I'm not proud to admit this, but I resented her for it. I remember being so hurt for a few days following that I wanted to make her do more chores than she already had, just to show her how hurt and disappointed I was. I know, that's terrible, and it hurts my heart just typing those words, but that was my first response.

Needless to say, I've matured since that day, and I've learned not to place expectations or dreams on my kids that aren't their dreams, but to guide them toward God's path for their lives. I've also learned that, like adults, kids can sometimes say things that aren't meant to hurt us, but they still do. She wasn't trying to intentionally hurt me, but she did. Either way, I had no right to hold that against her. I remember God rebuking me by telling me to repent of my wrongful resentment and ask for her forgiveness—so I did.

I bet that I'm not the only one who has been deeply disappointed and hurt by another person. Maybe, like me, one of your kids has hurt you? Maybe a friend at school? Or maybe you've been hurt by your parents?

Forgiving My Cowgirl

While all hurt is not equal and some of the people we love the most can hurt us the most, *who* hurt us really isn't the point. What matters is our *response* to the offense. Like me, you can respond poorly and want to make them pay. Or you can respond like Jesus by quickly forgiving them of the offense. Know this, if you don't *release* forgiveness, you won't *receive* forgiveness. Matthew 6:14-15 says, "If you forgive those who sin against you, your heavenly Father will forgive you. But if you refuse to forgive others, your Father will not forgive your sins" (NLT). What God is saying here is that to not forgive is unforgiveable. What God expects of us is for us to forgive those who hurt us, whether it was intentional or unintentional. If we do, God says He will forgive us. If we don't, He says he won't forgive us. This just goes to show how big forgiveness really is. See, I wanted to hold a grudge against my daughter. But that's not pleasing to God.

The other thing that I've learned along the way is that we are called to love like we've never been hurt. Pastor Jentezen Franklin wrote a great book entitled *Love Like You've Never Been Hurt*. I recommend it to anyone who has ever been hurt, which, by the way, is all of us. God wants us to love everyone who has hurt us like we've never been hurt. You may be thinking, "There's no way I'm going to love them again. That would mean I'm saying that what they did to me was alright." No, loving them and forgiving them doesn't make what they did right, but it does make you right with God. Also, not everyone you forgive needs to be a part of your life. If someone abused you and you choose to forgive him or her, that doesn't mean you have to have a close relationship with them. It may be ok for you to love them from a distance. You may be saying to yourself, "Well, if they ask for my forgiveness, I'll forgive them." This isn't biblical either. We are to offer forgiveness even if they never ask for it (see Matthew 5:23-24).

Being hurt is a part of life, but God doesn't want us to stay hurt. He wants us to be healed, and, to experience healing, we must forgive. Fast-forward to now and all of my kids, including my daughter, beg to go work cattle and ride horses as much as possible. And I love it that they do.

CHEW ON THIS
Are you holding back your forgiveness from someone who hurt you? If so, make a call today. Set yourself free from the burden of unforgiveness.

PRAYER
Lord, thank you for forgiving me even though I've hurt you by choosing to sin. I open my heart to forgiving those who have hurt me, and I choose today to forgive them so I can

have a right relationship with you. Help me to love them like I've never been hurt.

DAY 37

Purple Sock

ACTS 20:35
In all things I have shown you that by working hard in this way we must help the weak and remember the words of the Lord Jesus, how he himself said, "It is more blessed to give than to receive." (ESV)

If you've ever been to a trade show where western tack is traded or sold, or even if you've just met up with a buddy to do a little trading, there's usually one item that a lot of cowboys use to carry their bits or spurs in. That item is a Crown Royal whisky bag, otherwise known as "the purple sock." Along with the whisky that comes in it, this famous bag has been around since 1939. The story behind this famous whisky and its purple sock is that when King George VI and his wife Queen Elizabeth visited Canada for the very first time, Crown Royal was gifted to them as

Purple Sock

a tribute to their royal visit.

You may be thinking, "Thanks, Beau, for the history lesson on whisky, but what's the point?" Well, not too long ago, Crown Royal came out with a new campaign slogan, "Live generously and life will treat you royally." From this slogan, they've gone on to make several commercials that encourage people to listen generously, serve others generously, welcome our troops home generously, and age generously. Out of this campaign, they've gone on to raise millions of dollars to give to charities and to support our troops overseas. It's interesting to note that Crown Royal has built their company on the foundation of being generous—first to the King and Queen of Britain, and today by giving generously to those who have served our country and to those in need. A person doesn't have to drink whisky to see the greatness of this campaign.

My point is, if a whisky company understands what it means to be generous, then I believe the church should also understand what it means to be generous. Actually, we shouldn't wait to be spurred on by another organization to be generous, but as the church we should be leading the way in our generosity towards those in need. After all, we are not selling "spirits," we are offering people new life through the power of the Holy Spirit. The truth is, when we are generous with our money, time, and talents, we're not showing our generosity to an earthly king, but to the King of kings and Lord of lords Himself! And guess what? He promises that if we will live generously toward Him and others, not only will life treat us royally, but He will too.

CHEW ON THIS
How generous are you with your money, time, and talents? Are you giving because you know it's the right thing to do or are you giving out of a cheerful heart? Are you giving the minimum required or are you giving above and beyond what's asked? Commit to God to truly be generous with what He has blessed you with. Don't waste your life only thinking about what you can do to get ahead yourself, but how you can use your resources to help others.

PRAYER
Lord, help me to be generous with the things you've given me. I want to offer my money, time, and talents to you today, and I pray that you will use whatever I have to bring you glory and help others.

DAY 38

The Scout

DEUTERONOMY 31:8
Do not be afraid or discouraged, for the LORD will personally go ahead of you. He will be with you; he will neither fail you nor abandon you. (NLT)

While most people would say that Augustus "Gus" McCrae is their favorite character in the miniseries *Lonesome Dove,* my favorite character is Joshua Deets. Played by Danny Glover, Deets's character is based off the real life of a former slave named Bose Ikard. After being freed by the Union victory and the Thirteenth Amendment, young Bose signed on to herd cattle for rancher and cattle driver Oliver Loving. After Loving is killed, Ikard remained in the service of Charles Goodnight, developing a bond with the famous cattleman that lasted a lifetime. After Ikard's death, Charles Goodnight paid tribute to his friend:

The Maker's Mark

> He was a good bronc rider and exceptional night herder, good with the skillet and pans, and surpassed any man I had in endurance and stamina. There was a dignity, a cleanliness, and a reliability about him that was wonderful. His behavior was very good in a fight, and he was probably the most devoted man to me I ever had. I have trusted him farther than any living man . . . We went through some terrible times during those four years on the trail. He was the most skilled and trustworthy man I had . . . He never shirked a duty.

In *Lonesome Dove,* Deets's job on the trail was being the scout. This meant that he'd ride ahead of the herd for miles, and sometimes days, scouting out the best path for the herd to take. He was responsible for finding where the nearest water was, knowing if there were any potential dangers ahead, and making sure it was safe to proceed. He'd then return and report to Captain Call and Gus what he'd found. For the cattle and the men, Deets's role meant the difference between success or failure and life or death.

Much like Deets's role as a scout, I believe that God is the ultimate scout. Today's key verse tells us that He will personally go ahead of us; He prepares the path we're to

The Scout

follow. He does this by not only equipping us with the knowledge of what path to take but also by promising to travel through it with us. He promises the spiritual refreshment we need along the way, and, like Deets, He's able to warn us of the dangers that lie ahead, protecting us from the assaults of our enemy, the devil. Personally, I love this about God. Why? Because often times, this ride we call life is built on faith. Meaning, we must step out, even when we can't see what's ahead, and trust that God has already scouted it out and that we have nothing to worry about. All we have to do is follow His trail.

For some of you, following His trail means that it's time for you to take a step of faith and trust Jesus with your life. This is what Jesus referred to as being born again (see John 3). To be born again means you take what you've learned about Jesus and you make it *personal*. You move from being religious to having a relationship with Him. To do this, you accept His free gift of forgiveness and receive eternal life through Him. This single decision is the most important decision you'll ever make and now's the time to make it.

For others of you, you've got the relationship, you're just not living a life of faith but one of fear. For you, following His trail means that you hand over your current situation, trust God's guidance, and follow His path. Speaking as one who's ridden with Christ for a while, I can person-

The Maker's Mark

ally attest that no matter what circumstance you are in, He understands it. And if you've taken a wrong turn, He knows how to get you back on the right path.

What is it that God is asking you to trust Him with? Is it the decision to start a family? A relationship He wants you to start or end? Maybe it's taking a step of faith and tithing for the first time? I can tell you from experience: God has seen what's ahead and He knows how to get you through it. You just have to trust the Scout.

CHEW ON THIS

What is God asking you to trust Him with today? What situation in your life has you full of fear and not faith? Have you handed Him your future? If no, why not?

PRAYER

Prayer of Salvation: *Jesus, I know I'm a sinner. I know that I've not trusted you with my life, but I want to change that right now. I'm giving you my life. Forgive me of my sins and come into my life. Thank you for not giving up on me and giving me eternal life. Amen.*

Prayer of Surrender: *Lord, I give you thanks for all the ways that you go before me and prepare my way. Today I want to step out in faith even when I don't know what's around the corner.*

DAY 39

Herd Animals

ROMANS 12:15-16
Be happy with those who are happy, and weep with those who weep. Live in harmony with each other. (NLT)

While John Wayne was right when he said, "The cow is nothing but trouble tied up in a leather bag," there is one thing cows understand well . . . community. Now I know that sounds weird, but it's true. Being herd animals, cows spend the majority of their time together. They graze, travel, sleep, and chew their cud together. This desire for community is never more apparent than when you try cutting one of them out of the herd. When you do this, you find out pretty quickly that they will try anything to get back to the herd. Or try stripping a yearling off the herd and penning it by itself. The isolated cow will ball, paw the ground, and walk the fence looking for a hole to get out of, all in an effort to get back to his buddies.

The Maker's Mark

Another way we know that cows value community is that cows tend to stick together when threatened. If you've ever been in a pen with a group of cows, and a dog enters the pen, you've probably seen a few cows join forces and try stomping the dog to death or chasing it out of the pen. Why? Because they want to protect their herd. Even a rogue cow that has the tendency of being a maverick will eventually rejoin the herd. Why? Because deep inside, cattle desire community.

Much like cows, I believe that God wants us to live in community. Sure, some of us like being alone more than others, but at the end of the day we need other people in our lives. You might think, "Well, I don't. I can experience all I need in life with God, on my own. Just give me a horse and a good dog, and I'm set!" I'm right there with you, but I would argue that while you don't need others around to experience life and the presence of God, you do need others around to fulfill His purpose.

It's God's will that we live in community for many reasons, but I want to point out a couple. First, we are able to use our spiritual gifts to grow Christ's kingdom. The church needs our gifts. For example, is your gift serving behind the scenes? The church needs people working behind the scenes all the time. If you're an extrovert, the church needs your outgoingness to make people feel comfortable and welcomed. By serving in and amongst

Herd Animals

others, you give yourself the opportunity to change lives. And I can tell you from experience, there is nothing better than having a front row seat to life-change.

Not only are we able to minister to others when we are in community, but, secondly, we can be ministered to as well. I've never heard a tree pray for me when I was in need (you may have, but you were probably smoking something you shouldn't have). My horse has never showed up and brought me food when I was sick or cried with me when I was hurting. But I have experienced these things from the church I'm in community with. Not to mention, when I've been attacked by someone or accused of something that's not true, I have yet to have the mountains defend my honor. But I have had people that I love and that love me defend me from certain haters.

Probably the most important part of being in community with other Christ-centered people is, when I go rogue and want to do something opposed to God's Word or try heading down a path that doesn't lead to righteousness, they are there to draw me back. They call me out. They speak the truth to me in love. And then they love me back into their community. It's been said, and I completely agree, "if you want to go fast, go alone. If you want to go far, go together."

The Maker's Mark

CHEW ON THIS

Do you have a Christ-centered community that you are a part of? If no, why not? Are you committed to going to church so that your family can have community and support? When was the last time you used your gifts to serve others in the name of Jesus?

PRAYER

Jesus, I don't want to do this life alone. Help me to do my part in developing relationships with others, so that we can see people's lives changed for your glory. Bring me the friendships I need to succeed in life.

DAY 40

King George's Encore

1 CORINTHIANS 2:9
No eye has seen, no ear has heard, and no mind has imagined what God has prepared for those who love him. (NLT)

I've had the pleasure of seeing George Strait in concert and I can attest that it's nothing short of magical. When he walks out on that stage, the crowd just loses it. It's unlike anything I've ever seen. Girls screaming, guys raising their bottles, and when George starts singing one of his sixty number-one hits, it's like you're living in a scene from the movie *Pure Country*. It's awesome! Songs like, "All My Ex's Live in Texas," "Amarillo By Morning," "Troubadour," "Run," "Give It Away," "Baby Blue," "The Chair," and the list goes on and on. But while I like all of his songs, I'm particularly fond of one you may have never heard. It's entitled "El Rey," and George sings this song in Spanish on his twenty-sixth studio album *Twang*. I inherited my love for Spanish music from my father, and I'm glad I did. The words "El Rey" stand for "The King," which I would say is fitting for King George.

At a George Strait concert, when King George sings what seems to be his last song of the night and walks off the stage, most fans know that this is not the end of the concert. What happens next is what's known as the encore. This is when George comes back out and sings a few more of his best songs. It's amazing to listen and watch as the crowd goes nuts while he's off stage, and then when he returns to the stage they go even more nuts. Why? Because he saved the best for last.

Although no artist can match a King George encore, there is an encore that no one has ever seen yet. An encore like no other encore ever performed. What encore am I talking about? The encore of the one true King—King Jesus! See, He's come once already and He performed some great miracles while He was here. He turned water into wine, healed the sick, fed 5,000 people with a few loaves of bread and a couple fish ... not to mention ... He rose from the dead. Yeah, He's that guy!

But after performing these and other miracles, He left his earthly stage and returned to His home in heaven.

King George's Encore

Sad, I know! But, before He left, He promised us an encore. See, He promised that He was going to return and perform even greater miracles than He did earlier. Miracles like getting rid of the old earth and heaven and making new ones (Revelation 21:1). Miracles like raising people out of their graves and giving them new bodies (John 5:28-29, 2 Corinthians 5:3). (Praise God—I'm asking for my six pack back.) As if that weren't enough, we will also be taken up to witness the greatest concert of all in heaven. There, we will experience something that, as our key verse tells us, no eye has ever seen, nor ear has ever heard. No more tears, pain, sickness, or evil. No more singing off-key or guitar strings breaking! Just complete perfection!

So, the question becomes: What are we to do while waiting for the encore? Well first, we have to get our tickets. What I mean is, we have to accept Jesus into our hearts, be forgiven of our sins, and receive entry into the concert of eternity. You may ask, "How much are tickets?" Well, the cool thing is, Jesus has already paid for them. We just have to pick them up at the will call, where all He asks is that we call upon His name and confess Him as our Lord and Savior. That's what gets us in. Then, just like what happens at a George Strait concert right before the encore, we are to go nuts in worship and praise Jesus while waiting for His return to the earth. This means that we live for Him in every area of our lives. We worship Him at church, in our homes, with our kids, with our money—with everything. Are you ready?

CHEW ON THIS
Are you ready for Jesus' encore? Have you placed your trust in Him? Are you living in a way that you will be proud of when He returns? What must you start doing to get ready?

PRAYER
Jesus, I want to be ready for your return. I commit to worship you in every area of my life. Show me where I'm not ready and give me the strength to get ready. I look forward to seeing you return to the stage.

NOTES

NOTES